Presentation Skills
for Managers

Other titles in the Briefcase Books series include:

To learn more about titles in the Briefcase Books series go to
www.briefcasebooks.com

A Briefcase Book

Presentation Skills for Managers

Second Edition

Kerri Garbis

McGraw Hill Education

New York Chicago San Francisco Athens
London Madrid Mexico City Milan New Delhi
Singapore Sydney Toronto

1 2 3 4 5 6 7 8 9 QFR/QFR 21 20 19 18 17 16

ISBN   978-1-259-64396-5
MHID   1-259-64396-4

e-ISBN   978-1-259-64397-2
e-MHID   1-259-64397-2

Library of Congress Cataloging-in-Publication Data

Names: Garbis, Kerri, author.
Title: Presentation skills for managers / Kerri Garbis.
Description: Second edition. | New York : McGraw-Hill Education, 2016.
Identifiers: LCCN 2016024414 (print) | LCCN 2016027480 (ebook) | ISBN
    9781259643965 (paperback : alk. paper) | ISBN 1259643964 | ISBN
    9781259643972 ()
Subjects: LCSH: Business presentations. | BISAC: BUSINESS & ECONOMICS /
    Business Communication / Meetings & Presentations.
Classification: LCC HF5718.22 .G37 2016 (print) | LCC HF5718.22 (ebook) | DDC
    658.4/52--dc23
LC record available at https://lccn.loc.gov/2016024414

This is a CWL Publishing Enterprises book developed for McGraw-Hill Education by CWL Publishing Enterprises, Inc., Madison, Wisconsin, www.cwlpub.com.

Product or brand names used in this book may be trade names or trademarks. Where we believe there may be proprietary claims to such trade names or trademarks, the name has been used with an initial capital or it has been capitalized in the style used by the name claimant. Regardless of the capitalization used, all such names have been used in an editorial manner without any intent to convey endorsement of or other affiliation with the name claimant. Neither the author nor the publisher intends to express any judgment as to the validity or legal status of any such proprietary claims.

McGraw-Hill Education products are available at special quantity discounts to use as premiums and sales promotions, or for use in corporate training programs. To contact a representative, please visit the Contact Us pages at mhprofessional.com.

Contents

Acknowledgments

While it may be my name on the cover, this book was a collaborative effort. The entire Ovation Communication team support was palpable during the process, and I will be forever grateful. This would not have been possible without the time, talent, humor, and energy of Richard Arseneault, Nick Verina, Tom Frey, and especially Bridget Beirne. Thank you to John Woods of CWL Publishing for trusting me with this project. It has been a joy and a fantastic learning experience. Many thanks to the calming influence of Eric Bergeron, whose belief in me and Ovation Communication has never faltered. Dedicated to Sydney Faye—look, Mama wrote a book!

Introduction

'm standing in the wings of my high school theater (The Baltimore School for the Arts)—a ballroom that once was part of an old hotel in Maryland. The stage looks like black ice, and I'm afraid I'm going to slip. I hear the audience talking (it's a packed house). My castmates are fussing around me. Men are wearing puffy pirate shirts, and women with nearly identical flowing, curly hair are wearing long black skirts. I hear the orchestra warming up and the "tap, tap, tap" of the conductor's baton on his music stand. The overture is about to begin.

I start to panic. My heart pounds, I can barely breathe. My vision gets cloudy, and I'm pretty sure I'm dying. I think my feet are stuck. I have to go on stage, right now, but I'm only wearing my bathrobe, not my costume. Worst of all, I don't know my lines, or even what show I'm doing. My high-school musical-theater teacher pushes me hard on the back, and I stumble onto the stage. That's the last thing I remember.

Good thing this is just me having another actor's nightmare.

Why Consider the Actor's Perspective?

Ask any actors about their classic actor's nightmare and they probably will share some similar themes. It somehow involves a lack of preparation. At our core, actors are masters of preparation. Even on the improv stage, when the act is spontaneous, the actors are still prepared. Preparation is what we learn first and foremost in our training. It's so important that in my undergraduate studies (I received a BFA in musical theater from Syracuse University), we weren't permitted to perform in any shows during our first year. We were there to concentrate on learning the fundamentals of our craft and eliminate any bad habits.

If one of the biggest reasons presenters feel nervous is a lack of preparation, then who better to learn from than masters of it? Actors! Actors know how to prepare. They also know how to execute. This is why you should consider this book as your go-to resource for presentation skills.

From my many years on the stage as an actor, and my years on stage as a professional speaker, I have put together the most important pieces to help you become a more engaging, confident presenter.

Technologically Speaking . . .

Anytime I talk about something shown on a screen, I refer to it as a visual. From my experience working in hundreds of different companies, from global conglomerates to start-ups, I've learned that each one of them has its own culture and standards when it comes to the aesthetics of their visuals. If I were to offer any guidelines or advice for your visuals, the results would be futile.

I will say this, with confidence, about visuals: less is more.

In my vast experience, no one has ever said, "I wish they had more visuals" or "I wish there had been more words, or bullets, or pictures on the slides." Remember, your visuals are there to enhance your presentation. They're not the star of the presentation—you are. This book will offer you many techniques for presenting with visuals, but I leave the content of those visuals up to you.

This Is a Book . . . and a Workbook

You'll find loads of useful tools in this book: a Blueprint to help you organize your content, a list of questions for better storytelling, and a worksheet for what I call Audience Analysis, just to name a few. For any interactive piece of content presented in a chapter, there's a fillable, blank template of the same piece in the Appendix. If they work for you, I encourage you to make copies and use them again and again.

This book will help you with all aspects of presentation preparation: the essentials of presentation skills, content creation, and of course, delivery techniques derived directly from the theater. All of these will help you really step up your game when preparing and presenting.

You're the Chef

One of my favorite things to do when not teaching, speaking, or acting is to cook. I own lots of cookbooks from all different eras and culinary styles. I can't seem to read enough about flavor combinations and techniques used by professionals. But I don't always follow the recipes to the letter. Sometimes I combine two or more recipes. Sometimes I'll read a few recipes just for inspiration and make up my own thing when I'm standing over my ingredients. My hope is that you'll use this book in the same way.

Try some of the techniques that are introduced in the chapters that follow and decide which "taste" the best. Explore which of the tools work for you. Ultimately, the dish—er ... presentation—you create will fit your taste and style perfectly.

The great chef Julia Child articulated the connection between cooking and acting beautifully when she said, "Drama is very important in life: You have to come on with a bang. You never want to go out with a whimper. Everything can have drama if it's done right. Even a pancake." We won't spend any more time talking about cooking after this, but I do want to leave you with that image: trying different approaches and finding what you like best.

Acting is very personal. Presenting is, too. This book is yours. Use it as it works best for you.

Special Features

Titles in the Briefcase Books series are designed to give you practical information written in a friendly, person-to-person style. The chapters deal with tactical issues and include lots of examples. They also feature numerous sidebars that give you different types of specific information. Here's a description of the sidebars you'll find in this book.

Every subject has some jargon, including the field of presenting. The Key Term sidebars provide definitions of terms and concepts as they are introduced.

The Smart Managing sidebars do just what their name suggests: give you tips to manage the strategies and tactics described in this book.

Tricks of the Trade sidebars give you insider how-to hints on techniques speakers can use to execute the techniques described in this book.

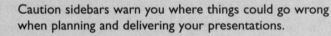

It's always useful to have examples that show how the principles in the book are applied. The For Example sidebars provide illustrations using the ideas included in this book.

Caution sidebars warn you where things could go wrong when planning and delivering your presentations.

How can you make sure you won't make a mistake when implementing the techniques this book describes? You can't, but the Mistake Proofing sidebars give you practical advice on how to minimize the risk of this happening.

The Tools sidebars provide things to use for implementing the techniques and ideas described in the book effectively.

Presentation Skills
for Managers

Chapter 1

The Rehearsal Process

I hope that you'll read this whole book and that you find numerous ideas and techniques that you can apply to your own presentations. But if you were to read only one chapter (and I'm not advocating that), this is the one to read. The reason is that nearly everything I have to offer you incorporates what I'm going to explain in the next few pages.

This chapter is about the Rehearsal Process, the method every actor uses in some way and has done since theater began. The Rehearsal Process is the bridge between good material and a great presentation. It is the link between the purely academic and the experiential. It gets your content out of your notes and into your body. Presentations don't happen on the page. They happen on a stage.

The material in this book is relatively easy to understand intellectually. You can read all of it, put it down, and say "Good, I got it." But leaving it there isn't going to work in any way toward making you a better presenter. Simply understanding what I'm saying isn't the point. You've got to find a way to apply it.

The solution is to use the Rehearsal Process. Actors spend years finding what works for them individually, but the essence of the process remains the same. The idea behind the Rehearsal Process is that you become so familiar with your material, and the challenges posed by presenting it, that no matter what is thrown at you, you can still deliver in a professional way.

Rehearsal Process The three-step technique actors have used throughout time to prepare for a production. From Sophocles to Shakespeare to Sondheim, the process holds.

KEY TERM

This process is also where you take the time to work on the fundamentals: the feet, the hands, the face, your vocal challenges, stage movement, and the rest. It's where you find out what works and what doesn't. In this regard, the Rehearsal Process actually influences content. Once you begin to lift your information off the page, it becomes clear very quickly what makes sense and what doesn't, what has impact and what's repetitive. Finding this out in the safety of rehearsal is much better than finding it out in front of an audience on the day of your presentation.

This technique has three steps: talk-through, walk-through, and dress rehearsal.

I encourage you to do each step more than once. Repetition of this process will help make all of your presentation choices second nature by building them into your muscle memory.

Muscle memory The result of the conscious repetition of a physical action, transferred into subconscious proficiency. If you do something over and over again, eventually you'll do it automatically and not have to think about it.

KEY TERM

This is an overview—I want you to get a feel for how the process works on a very high level. There are a lot of specifics that you can work on in each step of the Rehearsal Process. They're all covered in subsequent chapters. For now, get your mind used to thinking in these three steps.

The Talk-Through

On the first day of rehearsal for any play, the actors sit down with the director and simply read the entire play out loud. They just say all of the words the playwright wrote. Afterward they discuss, ask questions, and start the process of reading it again. This talking through of the play may occur multiple times before the actors ever get on their feet.

The first step of your Rehearsal Process is to simply talk through your presentation. Saying your content out loud helps you know what you actually mean. It gets you used to saying the words that will become your presentation. Your content doesn't have to be a finished product at this point. It can simply be a collection of notes.

TWO WAYS TO TALK THROUGH

When it comes to this first step, you can either:

1. Talk it out independently. You can certainly have a talk-through on your own. However, if you do, you've got to be diligent about not letting yourself off the hook. It *must* be out loud and at a good volume. Using your phone or other device to record and play back what you said helps keep the talk-through from reverting to a silent read-through.

2. Or, you can find a friend or colleague to sit down with you and listen. You're not so much looking for critique at this point but help in shaping what you have so far. It's useful to find someone who isn't as familiar with the material as you are, so that you get an idea of what your presentation will sound like to people not as well versed in it. You and your partner should both take notes to continue shaping your presentation.

Once you've talked through your presentation, you may benefit from another talk-through (or two or three) before you get on your feet.

TOOLS

This isn't about memorizing anything, but simply hearing it for the first time and getting a feel for what needs work. You may find that you need more content here and less there. Maybe you have too much content to fit the time you've been given (this is not uncommon). All this and more you can discover in your talk-through.

The Walk-Through

The second part of the Rehearsal Process is when you begin to put the material "on its feet." This is when you stand up and start to experiment with movement and gestures. Armed with the knowledge from your talk-through, you can now start to discover the physical shape of your presentation. Where might you move? Why would you do so? How can you use movement to highlight your ideas? This is an opportunity to make some big choices. You also have the luxury of finding out which movements work and which ones don't without any witnesses. You can work out all of your physical discomfort with presenting (Where do my hands *go*?) by yourself. At this point, your voice and articulators (I'll talk more

TRICKS OF THE TRADE

THE WALK-THROUGH AND SEATED PRESENTATIONS

Even if you're going to ultimately be presenting while sitting down, in a boardroom for example, it's important to use the walk-through. You might not be trying to discover stage movement, but you're still building awareness of your physicality when you say these words.

about them later . . .) will have found their way around your content, and you can let your body get comfortable with bold movement that supports your message.

I'll cover the nitty-gritty of stage movement, gestures, and more later in the book. For now, just know it's important at this step in the process to get moving.

Dress Rehearsal

The third step is the opportunity to give your presentation exactly as you will on the day, only without an audience. The point is to use everything you've learned in the talk-through and walk-through, with the addition of all of the technical elements and the clothes you plan on wearing.

SMART MANAGING

GET TO THE STAGE!

If possible, for your dress rehearsal, get into the space in which you will actually present. As a manager, encourage your team to do the same. Get everyone used to the idea of seeing "dress rehearsal" time blocked out on conference room schedules, etc. Make yourself available when you can for team rehearsals, and give your team the opportunity to show up to yours. When presentation skills are a subject of group discussion, you can see them improve across the board.

The ultimate goal of your dress rehearsal is to remove as many unknowns from your presentation as you possibly can. Really commit to doing this as you will in your final presentation. As with every point of the Rehearsal Process, this step doesn't have to be "one and done." It certainly can be if all you've got is one evening. However, you're welcome to have as many dress rehearsals as you have time for! If your first one gives you some good ideas as to what you could change, and you want to go back and give yourself another dress rehearsal, do it. It can't hurt.

The Rehearsal Process and You

By taking the time to do the talk-through, walk-through, and dress rehearsal, you're ensuring that you've done everything you can to eliminate the unnecessary, to build on the good, and to make sure your fundamentals are working for you. You've gotten your presentation into your body so that you don't have to think about every element of it while you're presenting. As you continue to use it, I'm sure you'll uncover some of the other benefits of the Rehearsal Process as well. It's a great method for combating stage fright, for one thing.

There's something else important about the Rehearsal Process that I'll remind you of again and again throughout this book: the Rehearsal Process is time-flexible. So often, I hear people complain that they simply don't have the time (or don't want to make it) to practice their presentations. This is simply untrue. Whether you've got two days, two weeks, or two months, you can adjust this process timewise to work for you. Each rehearsal doesn't have to take hours and hours, but it can if you have the time. On an extremely brief schedule, even giving each step a matter of minutes can make the difference.

That said, if you really want to improve, if you really want to present like a pro, you've got to put the time in. If you've got time to really go in depth with the Rehearsal Process, you absolutely should. Use it to your advantage. This is what makes the difference between average and outstanding presentations.

Don't Quit Your Day Job

One summer, I worked at the Weathervane Theatre in Whitefield, New Hampshire. The theater presented its season of shows in repertoire, meaning every night, each week, the theater presented a different show or musical. This was great for the family whose vacation in the White Mountains only spanned a week. It was pretty tough on the actors who were rehearsing one, or possibly two shows during the day and performing another one at night. The only way I got through that summer was by executing a well-organized Rehearsal Process.

My point is, if I can take the time to rehearse and do my preparation work while performing another show or two, I know you can make time—even if it's just a few minutes per day.

Can You Rehearse Too Much?

A lot of time dedicated to rehearsal, to some people, means their delivery will be inauthentic or boring. But rehearsal is not just mindless repetition or memorization of canned movements and vocal choices. It's about experimenting to find what works best. If you rehearse by saying the same things over and over again and doing the same things over and over again, then, yes, you can rehearse too much. If you rehearse in a smart way that helps you improve with each talk-through, walk-through, or dress rehearsal, then you can never be overrehearsed.

I'm not asking you to become an actor. However, I am asking you to think like one. No actor I know would dream of taking the stage in a play or musical without some kind of rehearsal. To be a masterful presenter, neither should you.

Manager's Checklist for Chapter 1

☑ Embrace the Rehearsal Process!

☑ The talk-through
- Remember to say your presentation out loud.
- Your presentation content doesn't have to be completely finalized.
- Get used to saying the words and discovering what content works and what doesn't.

☑ The walk-through
- Talk through your presentation on your feet.
- Experiment with stage movement, gestures, and more.
- Start to build muscle memory.

☑ Dress rehearsal
- The only thing absent from this rehearsal is the audience!
- Use all of your visuals, your wardrobe, everything.
- Invite colleagues, if possible, for an extra outside opinion.

☑ Remember, the Rehearsal Process is time-flexible. You *can* make it work for you!

☑ Don't fret about overrehearsing. Rehearse smart to keep things fresh.

Chapter 2

The Essentials

The first step in improving your presentation skills is becoming aware of how you present now. This chapter is designed to help you do that. Some things you do are really good already; some other things might need attention. Finding which skills to feature, and which to fix, is the beginning. Your body language, your eye contact, and your vocal production all contribute to how you're being perceived and how powerfully you can deliver your message.

The Feet, the Hands, and the Face

Becoming aware of, and eliminating, something you've been doing for a long time can be an odd sensation. I encourage you to live with that strangeness for a while, with the promise that you'll be rewarded with a greater control of the information you're giving off.

I've broken the body down into three areas: the feet, the hands, and the face. By "feet," I mean your posture in general as well as movement around the stage. By "hands," I mean gestures, and by "face," I mean facial expressions and engagement.

Feet

How you move and stand can positively or negatively affect the delivery of your message. Few of us are naturally aware of our habitual resting posture until someone points it out or we see ourselves on camera. While habits like leaning into one hip, clasping your hands behind your back, crossing your ankles, etc., aren't necessarily offensive, they do give off information and can distract from your message (See Figure 2-1.)

The way to solve any of these ineffective habitual stances is to replace them with another one. I call it Neutral Position.

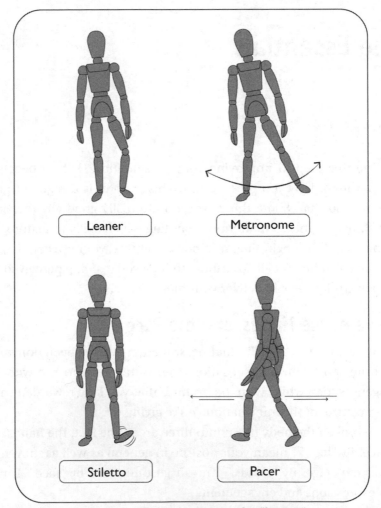

Figure 2-1. Four ineffective habitual stances: The "leaner" spends time sunk into one hip or the other; the "metronome" shifts weight continuously back and forth between the feet; the "stiletto" puts weight on one foot while shaking the foot from the heel of the other; the "pacer" stalks back and forth across the space.

Neutral Position is a presenter's balanced, default position that helps ensure that the presenter projects only the information he or she chooses to the audience. It also conveys comfort and confidence. It's not meant to be a static position but one that you can return to from time to time during your presentation (Figure 2-2).

When I teach this position to people they often say, "This feels weird," and I agree. It felt weird to me too when I first started practicing it. We're just not used to being there. Neutral Position is most likely not your "natural position," but a stance a presenter develops. I encourage you to try it out and let it feel strange for a while until it feels natural.

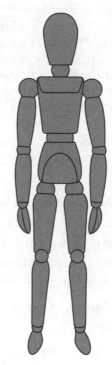

Figure 2-2. A strong Neutral Position

Remember, this is not a position that you're stuck in throughout your presentation. It's simply one of many positions your body will take.

In order to feel comfortable and confident in Neutral Position, it helps to practice it outside of the stress of a presentation. Some good places are waiting in line at the bank, grocery store, airport, or coffee shop. No one will know....

BEWARE OF SHRINKING

Being up in front of people is tough, and our bodies generally want to get smaller or go away. You may see people crossing all of their limbs, rolling their shoulders in, or practically crouching in an effort to hide away from the crowd. This unconscious shrinking is a detriment to your credibility with an audience.

Don't be afraid to open up and inhabit your own space! You're worth it. Simply opening your physicality will help you garner confidence and trust from your audience.

FINDING YOUR NEUTRAL POSITION

Here's how to do it: Stand with your feet about shoulder width apart, hips centered, chest high, arms by your side, chin parallel to the ground. Now, raise your arms over your head and let them

TOOLS   drop back down to your sides. That's it. Where they land, and where your body is now, is your Neutral Position. Get up and give it a try!

You can also use your strong Neutral Position when seated. Keep your feet flat on the floor, your shoulders back, and your head aligned. Keep your hands and arms above the table, however; no need to leave them at your sides. This is a great place to work from for seated presentations (Figure 2-3).

Make a Plan for Stage Movement

Movement around the stage is useful and engaging. However, when done without purpose, it can be pointless and distracting. I'm going to spend a whole chapter discussing effective stage movement, but for now, let me say this: A good rule of thumb is if you

Figure 2-3. Seated Neutral Position

don't have to move, don't. Sometimes, I see people pacing during their presentations. They stalk the floor from side to side, striding like a general or a caged animal. I believe they think they are generating excitement or conveying a sense of urgency, but to me they seem like they're trying to find a way to escape. I don't think it means what they think it means.

If you need to move, plan it. If you want to get out of the way of the screen, good. If you are using spots on the stage to correlate to ideas that you revisit, good. If you are using movement to represent passage of time, etc., good. The rule, again, is this: unless you have a reason to go over there, don't. Stay where you are. The audience needs to hear what you have to say, and this is the first time they've heard it. If you're wandering or pacing, you're undercutting your message. Once you've synthesized the idea of purposeful, content-related movement, where one supports the other, it's wonderful. However, doing it in an unplanned or unconscious way is just distracting.

Hands

Much like stage movement, gestures can be an asset or a liability. Open, confident gestures enhance your presentation with clarity, interest, and energy. Closed, indistinct, or ineffective physical habits detract from your content. They also lower credibility, suggest nervousness, or connote lack of interest in your own subject. I've seen presenters undercut really interesting content with bad or repetitive gestures.

Figure 2-4 shows some common, ineffective physical habits to recognize and avoid.

Some general rules to follow are that good gestures are ones that are fully committed, made above the hips, with the elbows away from the body (this avoids "T-rex" arms). But what does it really mean to fully commit to a gesture?

When presenting, the thought behind these gestures, and the desire to make them, won't change. What will change is the scale. If you're presenting in a large venue, you want to keep your gestures bigger to balance the size of your stage. Of course, if you're presenting around a table, use your discretion. While gestures in a small space might be smaller themselves, they shouldn't be any less distinct.

DEALING WITH PROPS

TRICKS OF THE TRADE

There are lots of handheld items you may use during a presentation: perhaps a remote to control visuals, or a clipboard you'll reference, or something to enhance a personal story. We'll refer to them collectively as props.

Feel free to use props, with this caveat—if you're going to hold them, you've got to use them then put them down when you're through. This means no holding a pen simply to keep your hand occupied, or clinging to a remote when you don't need to change a slide, or aimlessly rifling through pages on a clipboard. All of this tells the audience that you're nervous and simply looking for something to do with your hands. Just like movement, if you choose to hold a prop, it must be for a purpose.

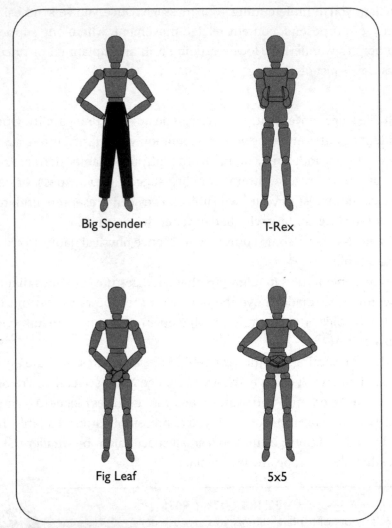

Figure 2-4. Four examples of ineffectual gestures: "Big spenders" hide their hands in their pockets; the "T-rex" keeps elbows connected to the waist, leaving only half an arm to gesture with; "fig leaf" is hands clasped low, in front of you; and the "5x5" is the matchup of the fingertips on each hand, often used to gesture as a unit.

We all fully commit to gestures every day: when we're describing something really big or really small; when we celebrate booking a big client; when we bury our head in our hands to cry. We use big, connected, *real* gestures constantly.

No Need for Recital Arms

I want you to think about gestures and experiment with ones that feel good during your Rehearsal Process, while eliminating your personal bad habits. I love gestures. They're important. But keep this thought in mind: I'm not asking you to memorize gestures on certain words or to use a certain gesture at the same time every single time. (Although that can sometimes be fun when used for humor or storytelling . . .)

The goal of emphasizing attention to gestures is to help you free yourself to use bold, supportive hand and arm movements that won't accidentally undermine your content. It's not to make you resemble your ten-year-old niece in her dance recital. Never fear when I'm asking you to be bold and work on your gestures. Keep them strong, open, and free, and you'll never feel "over-played."

Face

Facial expressions are made up of an incredibly complex interplay of facial muscles.

While some expressions are made consciously, many more are made unconsciously, arising out of what we are feeling in any moment. While we can't control all of our facial expressions, becoming aware of potential negative habits is essential.

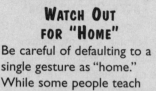

Watch Out for "Home"

Be careful of defaulting to a single gesture as "home." While some people teach that you should return to the "5x5" or even the "fig leaf," remember: everything says something. Do you really mean to be saying whatever it is over and over again? Or is it just a habit that feels safe? Challenge yourself to come back to Neutral Position instead.

Among the facial expressions we can control, simply smiling is a good place to start. A casual smile is appropriate for nearly any message. Unless you are delivering bad news, why not?

Making Eye Contact Work for You

Along with awareness of our expressions, good eye contact is the most immediate way to foster connection and increase credibility with your audience. Smiling and making eye contact doesn't come naturally to everyone, however. In the beginning, it may seem awkward or even

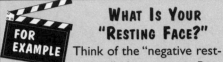

WHAT IS YOUR "RESTING FACE?"

Think of the "negative resting face" phenomenon. People who unconsciously default to this expression often think they appear open and engaged while listening, when in fact they look negative or judgmental. Fixing it may be as simple as practicing in a mirror or asking the assistance of a trusted colleague. Becoming aware of your "resting face" or other habits can help avoid sending mixed messages to your audience.

THREE-SECOND ZONE

Three seconds is the guideline for keeping an appropriate amount of eye contact. If you're holding it for less than three seconds, you may **TOOLS** appear shifty or distracted. If you keep it for longer than that, it's . . . creepy.

insincere, but with work it will start to feel more natural, connective, and authentic. The key to comfortable eye contact for all involved lies in knowing how long to hold it.

Regardless of the size of your presentation audience, eye contact comes into play. When in a small group, you'll want to move your gaze around the room, catching the eyes of everyone at different times. If you've got a large audience, you still need to make as much eye contact as you can. Sometimes, due to bright stage lights or especially big crowds, you may only be able to try to focus on one part of a large section at a time. Do your best, but don't abandon the idea completely.

If you struggle with this, you can begin by practicing a casual smile and relaxed eye contact in all your interactions. If you can learn to use these tools in a nonpressurized situation, it will be that much easier to use them while presenting.

Empowering Your Voice

In terms of vocal production, the beginning of using your voice well is understanding the relationship between breath and vocal support. Whether presenting in a large hall or a boardroom, or even on the phone, good vocal production is vital. This isn't possible without good breath support. This includes when you're using a microphone. Any sound designer will tell you that the mic is there to support, not create the voice.

While all of us breathe in a perfectly acceptable manner for remaining alive, some of us don't breathe effectively for good vocal production. Shallow breathing or a breath that causes tension, around the voice or otherwise is counterproductive. The easiest way to counteract this is to practice what is called the "core breath."

A good thing to note about volume is that it's better to be a little too loud than to not be heard. If you are too loud, which is extremely rare, the audience will let you know (either verbally or nonverbally). It's better to err on the side of greater volume, rather than have parts of your audience miss out on your message.

TRY THIS EXERCISE WITH YOUR TEAM!

SMART

MANAGING

Have one person tell a brief story to everyone (how she got to work that day, what she had for dinner last night, e.g.). The goal is to keep eye contact with each person for no more and no less than three seconds.

Tell the rest of the team to raise their hand at the beginning of the story. When the person telling the story makes eye contact with any one of them, the audience member must silently count to three before putting his hand down. If the storyteller moves on before that, that person keeps his hand raised until he's been given a full three seconds of eye contact.

Listen not only for volume but for variety. Just as we all have habits of posture, we also have habits of pitch. By pitch, I mean the music in your voice, the highs and lows. A varied use of it attracts and holds audience

---

CORE BREATHING

TOOLS

Try this exercise. This is one you probably *shouldn't* do while waiting in line at the bank or airport or coffee shop ...

In a standing position, put one of your hands on your lower abdomen. Inhale through your nose on a count of five, and feel your stomach push against your hand. Your shoulders shouldn't move, and your neck shouldn't tense. Exhale on the syllable "ahhh," nice and loud. Repeat a few times. That amount of breath is what's available for your support every time you speak.

Of course, we don't always have a count of five to inhale, so practice releasing into it more quickly as you learn. That much breath has a lot of other benefits as well which I'll get to later. For now, see how it can affect your vocal production, particularly in terms of volume, pitch, and clarity.

KEY TERMS

Monotone Using only one pitch (and volume) throughout. It's the least interesting way of delivering content.

Down-speak Lowering your pitch at the end of every phrase. In the theater, it's known as "throwing away the end of your lines." As an occasional technique to indicate *gravitas* it may be useful, but as a habit, it connotes a complete lack of interest or energy.

Up-speak Raising your pitch at the end of every phrase, making every sentence sound like a question. People who use it habitually seem to lack credibility, no matter how brilliant the content being delivered.

interest and can add to their understanding of your content. The Key Terms give you some vocal patterns to look out for.

The third major area of speech is articulation. Your words lose all value if your audience can't understand you. Clarity in articulation is essential, from start to finish. Some common pitfalls are the following:

- **Swallowing Initial Consonants.** "This is ..." becomes "'is is," "That's how we ..." becomes "'at's how we," etc. Often the presenter isn't using enough volume at the beginning of the sentence, so the audience doesn't hear any content until the second word.
- **Running Words Together.** "I'm going to ..." becomes "Ahmanah," and "Did you ..." becomes "Didja," and so forth.
- **Lack of Final Consonants.** "Goin'," "Somethin'," "Seein'," etc. The proper use of a final consonant helps make your point very clearly, even if at first it feels overdone.

As you're becoming aware of, and modifying, some of these habits, I can understand if you start to wonder if there is any "you" left in how you speak. Vocal identity is a very personal thing. Changing parts of it, even if those parts are in your way, is really hard. There's one area that I don't think you need to change, however. Some people think we need to strive to get rid of our regionalisms, our accents. I don't agree. All of us have an accent of some kind, whether we think so or not. Particularly strong accents or regionalisms are only a barrier if they keep us from being understood. As long as the words and meaning are clear, the particular, genuine sound of where you come from may be considered part of your personality. Keep your accent. It's yours. The more confident we feel about how we speak, the more credible we seem.

SLOW DOWN

When some people are nervous, the pace of their speech increases and they're off to the races! When people speed through their words, ramble away, or run things together, it's nearly impossible for an audience to catch their meaning.

A speaker that's too slow is rare; however, rapid speech is far more common. If you struggle with this, breath, articulation, and eye contact can help. Not only are core breaths good for a dose of calm, but the time it takes to use them helps you slow your speech overall. When you truly articulate all of your words, it acts as a mini–brake system. It's difficult to speed through your content when you're saying each and every word clearly. Lastly, good eye contact gives you a focal point; rather than rambling away, you bring back the feeling of a one-on-one conversation.

VOCAL CARE

Take care of your voice in the time leading up to your presentation. Here are some tips on how to do that:

- **Stay Hydrated.** Drink plenty of water the day of, and day before, a presentation. Dehydration can seriously impact vocal production.
- **Vocal Rest.** Consider how you use your voice the night before and day of the presentation. The voice uses muscles that can get tired like any others. Shouting at a ball game or a noisy restaurant the night before can cost you the next day.
- **Avoid Caffeine.** Coffee and tea are diuretics and at the least can contribute to extra nerves.

Avoiding Filler Words

I want to give you a tip that can help you become a better presenter right away: get rid of Verbal Viruses. Verbal Viruses are meaningless filler words or sounds that detract from the delivery of your content. The most common is "um," but there are many, many more.

You may not even know you're doing some of them. Start listening for them in other people and see if you're guilty of any of them yourself. The solution? Replace them with a pause. The pause gives you a moment to think and choose your words. It can also pique the interest of the people listening to you.

CAUTION

**DON'T SPREAD
A VERBAL VIRUS!**

Here are some common
filler words that our speech
may be riddled with:

"Ummm ..."

"You see ..."

"... and"

"... but"

"You know what I mean?"

"Ahhhh ..."

"Look ..."

"You know ..."

"Such as ..."

These are your presentation essentials. They're the basic foundations of a good presentation. They take practice and commitment, but nothing I've told you here is impossible or mysterious. You can do it. Tackle them a piece at a time, slowly putting them all together until they're so engrained in your body that they're second nature.

**TRICKS
OF THE
TRADE**

ONE BITE AT A TIME

Practice your "pause" and the elimination of your Verbal Viruses in small bites. If you choose your next two-hour presentation as the time you'll pause every time you have the urge to use an "um," you're going to fail. Start infusing pauses, in lieu of "ums," into your speech by practicing on a brief call or sharing a short story with a friend. When you're first getting started, let the listener know what you're doing. With lots of urges to "um," and therefore lots of pauses, your story may come out slower than usual. Get the habit of pausing into your muscle memory, and before you know it, you'll barely have to think about it.

Manager's Checklist for Chapter 2

☑ Spend time on your presentation physicality: the feet, hands, and face.

  ■ Discover your ineffective stances, as well as your own Neutral Position.

  ■ Experiment with bold, supportive gestures while eliminating distracting ones.

  ■ Ask yourself if your facial expressions are communicating something other than what you intend, and smile (unless you're delivering bad news!).

☑ Make eye contact work for you.
- Get comfortable with making eye contact for three seconds, and practice!
- Recognize that it's important in presentations, as well as conversations.

☑ Empower your voice.
- Use pitch, articulation, and volume to your advantage.
- Develop your breath support through core breathing.

☑ Avoid filler words
- Pause instead of uttering a Verbal Virus.
- Practice, over time, speaking without filler words.

Fear and Confidence

Many of the greatest actors throughout history have dealt with stage fright. Actors are humans, after all. Countless celebrities have reported suffering from this very human struggle. Stage fright is so prevalent, in fact, that you've undoubtedly heard the old trope that many people fear public speaking more than death itself. It's that bad. Countless actors and speakers, yours truly included, at times, tremble at the thought of standing before an audience. Yet, we continue to perform because we have tools we can use to handle the fear.

In this chapter, we'll discuss the ins and outs of the fear of public speaking, or stage fright. We'll talk about how you can learn to live with, and maybe even come to appreciate, those unbearable nerves that creep in before you present.

Why Am I Nervous?

There are lots of phobias: arachnophobia (fear of spiders), kleptophobia (fear of stealing), geniophobia (fear of chins—yes, that's a real thing), and on and on. Just like these, the fear of public speaking is another phobia, and it's closely connected with performance anxiety.

Stage fright is nothing to be embarrassed about. It shouldn't make you feel ashamed. Think about it: there's a lot that's daunting and frightening about standing and speaking in front of others! Actors often worry that they might forget their lines, that the audience won't like their work,

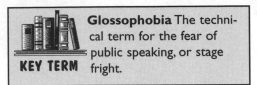

Glossophobia The technical term for the fear of public speaking, or stage fright.

KEY TERM

or that if they give a poor performance, it could spell the end of their career. Sound familiar?

Whether you're giving a large or a small presentation, it's easy to see why you might get nervous. What if your boss isn't pleased with your work? What if the audiesce doesn't ike how you look? What if you don't have the answers to everything? What if ... What if ... What if! That sinking, often cyclical, feeling of anxiety over your performance should never make you feel inadequate. On the contrary, it shows how deeply you care about what you do. While your self-esteem may be suffering, learning more about what's actually happening in your body, and how to deal with it, can help.

The root of your nerves is found in one of the body's most basic reactions: the "fight or flight" response we feel in the face of fear. Our bodies still respond the same way they did ages ago when confronted with a threat from a large animal, eager to make us his dinner. The body releases the hormone adrenaline, and we get ready to make the decision between duking it out with our enemy or running for our lives.

Luckily, there's not a saber-toothed tiger waiting for anyone at the end of his or her presentation. However, the adrenaline release related to stage fright can feel just as bad. Your breathing may become rapid, your mouth may dry out. You may start to shake or sweat or feel light-headed. All of this can be connected back to the hormonal change in your body.

"Why am I nervous?" This question can have many answers when it comes to stage fright. Whatever your personal responses may be, they're all rooted in a feeling of anxiety over your performance, with physical reactions spurred on by our body's fight or flight response.

Saying, "I just need to calm down!" isn't going to help. That's like telling yourself not to think about a purple rhinoceros. Once you say that, it's all you can think about. Don't fight this fear or be shamed by it. Acknowledge that it's real so you can take steps to deal with it.

Harnessing Your Nerves

So, you're nervous. How can you accept your fear and yet move ahead with your public speaking? There are two levels of the approach to harnessing your nerves and eventually feeling calm and confident for your presentation: the work you will do in advance and the work you will do just before you go on.

The Advance Work

The best way—the *very* best way—to deal with stage fright is through preparation. Those nagging "What if?" questions that we discussed above can drive the cycle of performance anxiety, and preparation can help you put them to rest. As you rehearse your presentation, using the Rehearsal

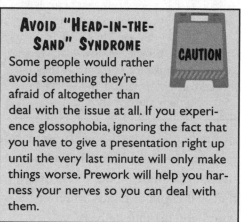

AVOID "HEAD-IN-THE-SAND" SYNDROME

CAUTION

Some people would rather avoid something they're afraid of altogether than deal with the issue at all. If you experience glossophobia, ignoring the fact that you have to give a presentation right up until the very last minute will only make things worse. Prework will help you harness your nerves so you can deal with them.

Process, you'll be able to eliminate many of your presentation unknowns far in advance.

Just as Rome wasn't built in a day, your presentation shouldn't be either! The important thing is that you start mapping out your Rehearsal Process as soon as you find out that you're expected to give a presentation.

Each part of the Rehearsal Process can help reduce stage fright. The more you get comfortable with giving your presentation through rehearsal, the better you'll be able to handle your performance anxiety.

KNOW YOUR TEAM

SMART

MANAGING

Do you have team members who struggle with public speaking? People who have exceptional ideas and input yet freeze when they have to communicate them? Encourage them to embrace the Rehearsal Process, and try to give them a little extra lead time when you'd like them to present. If possible, offer to check in with them along the way and see how their rehearsals are going. The more you can help them feel prepared and confident, the better they will be able to communicate their information.

Part 1: The Talk-Through

When you take the time to use the talk-through portion of your rehearsal, you accomplish two things: First, you get your articulators used to actually speaking the words you'll say. Second, each time you speak your presentation through, you get more and more familiar with your content itself.

> **Articulators** The parts of your body that actually help you speak and make **KEY TERM** sounds. They include your mouth, lips, tongue, and jaw. Just like any other musculature in the body, they need to be warmed up and worked out for optimum performance.

Fear of tripping over or mispronouncing words in a presentation can weigh heavily on a presenter. By simply sitting and talking through presentation content aloud, you can start to find a comfortable pace that allows you to speak your content in a way that can be understood. You get used to your rate of speech—something that will come in handy when in-the-moment nerves threaten to make you speed up your delivery.

Also, when nervous, the projection of your voice can suffer. You may experience dry mouth or shaky breathing, which can reduce your volume. During your talk-through, start to get accustomed to your presentation volume. Simply mumbling the words won't help; rehearsing them at full volume will. With each talk-through, you'll get your articulators used to the flow of the words you want to use and how it feels to say them. This may seem like a no-brainer, but ask

> **TRICKS OF THE TRADE**
>
> **WHAT'S IN A NAME?**
> If you've got a difficult name or two in your presentation, now's the time to reduce your fear of actually *saying* them by rehearsing. But first, make sure you have the correct pronunciation. Research how to say it, consult a colleague, or ask the person directly. People are always happy to help you pronounce their name correctly. Eliminate your fear of name failure by getting the correct pronunciation into your muscle memory during your talk-through.

anyone who's stumbled over critical information in a presentation how important getting it right can be!

The second useful side effect of the talk-through is familiarization with your content. There is no need for you to consciously attempt to memorize anything—save that for the actors! But each time you simply talk through your content, you become more closely connected with it. You learn the structure of your presentation: how things work, where they go. You'll have less fear about knowing what comes next in the moment, because you've talked it through so many times, from the first stage of the Rehearsal Process.

Part 2: The Walk-Through

Both actors and dancers often talk about the power of muscle memory. Training your body and your mind to remember a certain order of movements through repetition is at the core of performance for each of them. When you walk through your presentation during your rehearsals, you start to eliminate the physical fears wrapped up in presenting and build strong muscle memory in its place.

As we mentioned in "The Essentials," you can start to play with (and become accustomed to) strong, bold gestures. You can experiment with stage movement that you may want to use during your presentation and discover where it happens. Because you're doing all of this work in the safety of your private Rehearsal Process, you can make your

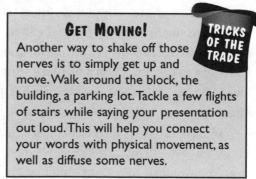

GET MOVING!
Another way to shake off those nerves is to simply get up and move. Walk around the block, the building, a parking lot. Tackle a few flights of stairs while saying your presentation out loud. This will help you connect your words with physical movement, as well as diffuse some nerves.

TRICKS OF THE TRADE

own mistakes, and find what works for you, without the pressure of an audience.

Part 3: The Dress Rehearsal

Your dress rehearsal is the perfect opportunity to tackle some of the lingering fears in your presentation: everything from "What will I wear?" to "What do I do if my visuals fail?" to "Is there anything I've missed in my rehearsals so far?"

Since the only thing absent from your dress rehearsal is the audience,

PREPARE TO PRESENT WITHOUT

Believe it or not, it's still possible to give a terrific presentation without any visuals at all. Should every solution and backup solution fail (hey, it's happened to me), the show must go on!

Acknowledge the situation, but avoid apologizing. Remember, no one knows what your presentation was supposed to look like. Actors know that one of the surest ways to sink a performance is to look like they're apologizing for the play.

Audiences love to see presenters triumph in the face of adversity, so forge ahead and be the hero. You'll make even more of a connection with your audience, and they won't forget seeing a true professional roll with the punches.

you should use everything else that you'll need for your presentation. Run all of your tech, whatever that may entail. The more comfortable you are with your tech, the less you'll have to worry about whether or not you know how to deal with it.

While dress rehearsal means *dress* rehearsal, if for some reason you can't wear your presentation clothing, at the very least, use your shoes. Usually in the first few days of rehearsal, actors receive the actual shoes they will be wearing during the performance. Getting comfortable in your footwear, in the space you'll be presenting, is extremely helpful when battling nerves. If you are unable to wear your entire "costume" for your dress rehearsal, at least wear your shoes.

Want to take your dress rehearsal to the next level? Invite a colleague to sit in. You'll get to practice how it will feel to look your audience in the eye and communicate directly to someone. You can even ask for his or her input and opinion on whether or not your presentation is clear and covers all the necessary bases. Having a vote of confidence and thoughts from someone you trust can help you feel more positive about your presentation.

How to Feel Calmer and Appear More Confident

In the time before your presentation, your body may shift into nervous overdrive. You may start to shake or have trouble breathing. You might feel a bit nauseated. The first thing to think about is regulating your breathing. The release of adrenaline can cause your breathing to become uneven. As a result, CO_2 can build up in the bloodstream, since it's not getting evenly expelled by measured breathing. This isn't a good thing! Breathing exercises help your body regulate the exchange of gases in the bloodstream, which will aid some of the discomfort your body is feeling.

Your breath is incredibly important when it comes to keeping calm before you go on. Start your warm-up by getting your breathing under control.

IN COLLEAGUES WE TRUST

CAUTION

There's a reason I always mention "trusted" colleagues when it comes to presentation rehearsals, especially if you're a person who struggles with stage fright. Invite someone who gives great input, with no ulterior motives. Does this mean you should shy away from criticism? Absolutely not. But find a colleague to work with who can keep all of his or her criticism constructive, rather than destructive. For stage fright sufferers, the right presentation "partner" can make all of the difference.

CORE BREATHING 2.0

TOOLS

In "The Essentials," I told you how core breathing was a necessary part of good vocal production. One of the other benefits of core breathing is that it's an integral part of the mind/body connection. When used in stressful situations like a presentation, it helps inform the brain that it isn't *really* in danger. This can limit the fight or flight response.

Here's core breathing for relaxation: revisit your core breathing, but now the focus will be on relaxing. Follow the steps for core breathing, only this time, inhale on a count of 10. When you hit your breath capacity, slowly release it out on a count of 10. Your shoulders should remain still; only your core and your hand should move. Repeat this process as needed to reduce nerves.

What can you do to control those twitchy muscles? Calm shakiness by engaging the muscles in question. You can warm up the muscles of your entire body by doing the warm-up below (Table 3-1):

- **Face:** Stretch out your face as much as you can; open your eyes and mouth wide. Then, quickly reverse it. Pull all your facial muscles in, furrowed brow, pursed lips. Alternate back and forth.

Head to Shoulders	Back to Feet
Face: big face/little face	Back: hug a tree
Jaw: chewing gum	Chest: crush an orange
Lips: race car	Arms: back stroke/circle
Tongue: tongue aerobics	Wrists: wrist circle
Neck: head rolls	Fingers: air piano
Shoulders: up/down/all around	Core: torso twist
Eyes: thumb/wall	Ankles: write your name

Table 3-1. The presenter's warm-up

- **Jaw:** Exercise your jaw by pretending to chew a piece of gum.
- **Face:** stretch your mouth, eyes, and jaw as wide as you can, then make them as small as you possibly can. Repeat three times each.
- **Eyes:** Extend your arm with one thumb raised. Focus on your thumb, then on the wall beyond it, to warm up your eye muscles.
- **Lips:** Blow air through your lips; some people may call this a "motorboat" sound.
- **Tongue:** Stick out your tongue. Move it up, down, and around the outside of your mouth.
- **Neck:** Gently roll your head from shoulder to shoulder and all the way around.
- **Shoulders:** Raise them up, drop them, and move them in circles.
- **Back:** Pretend you're hugging a wide tree to stretch your back muscles.
- **Chest:** Pretend to crush an orange between your shoulder blades.
- **Arms:** Do the "backstroke" in the air and some arm circles.
- **Wrists:** Gently move your wrists in circles, first one way, then the other.
- **Fingers:** Play the air piano! Pretend to move your fingers as fast as you can across an imaginary keyboard.
- **Core:** With arms out, bent at the elbows, do an easy torso twist.
- **Legs:** Shake out each leg, one at a time.
- **Ankles:** Use your foot to write your name in the air.

Take your time with these exercises; don't rush through them. (Remember to always use your discretion when it comes to physical activity.) What's great about this particular presenter's warm-up is that it can be done without much space at all! If you don't have a big empty conference room at your disposal, you can use any small, private space: the copy room, a stairwell landing, even a bathroom stall.

If you just sit there and shake, you're going to feel worse. Instead, get your muscles moving. Activate them to reduce the shakes. Couple this with your breathing for a double dose of calm.

Finding Your Mental Center

You've reined in your out-of-control physicality, but what can you do about your racing mind? Just as we did with our muscles, give your mind something to focus on other than your presentation for a bit. I like tongue twisters; they're a simple mental puzzle that gives your mind something to work on, while simultaneously warming up your articulators. It may seem silly, but just focusing on successfully saying "You know you need unique New York!" can take your mind away from the drowning mental cycle of impending doom that can creep in prepresentation.

LIST OF TONGUE TWISTERS

"A big black bug bit a big black bear and the big black bear bled blood."

"I slit a sheet, a sheet I slit, upon a slitted sheet I sit."

"Whether the weather be cold, or whether the weather be hot, we'll be together whatever the weather, whether we like it or not!"

"Peter Piper picked a peck of pickled peppers."

"You know you need unique New York."

TOOLS

You can also give your mind a few moments of mini-meditation. Often, in a guided meditation, you'll be asked to simply notice the sounds in the room around you. Let your mind go blank (or as close to it as possible!), close your eyes, and simply listen for a while. Really take note of what you hear: Are there any voices? Do you recognize them? Can you hear any whirring computer fans, or ringing phones? How about outdoor traffic, closing doors, or elevator bells? Let your brain focus on the noises surrounding you, and breathe. Becoming hyperaware of the world around you can turn your mind to something other than your mounting presentation anxiety.

I have a go-to activity when I'm looking to find my "mental center": I think about how I felt the last time I gave a successful presentation. When I'm nervous, I'll recall the who, what, where, and when of a good presenting experience. I try to relive how I felt after that presentation was over. Typically, I felt relieved, confident, and empowered. I was smiling. I tap into those memories just before I take the stage to present (or perform). This puts me in a positive mindset, and my nerves release their control. Try this technique for your next presentation.

Know Your Symptoms

When my sister asked me to sing at her wedding, I was honored. It was a beautiful wedding that took place at my parent's home in Baltimore. This was a small family gathering, just about 60 people. Even though it was a tiny crowd for me to sing in front of, I was *nervous*. It was her big day, and I wanted it to be perfect.

I warmed up and sang through my song in the morning before the ceremony. I was ready to go. Happily, the song and ceremony went well. I was glad I'd done a good job for my sister's special day.

Just after the ceremony, a cousin stopped and asked me, "Are you allergic to flowers?" I told him, "No, I'm not allergic to anything." He looked at me inquisitively and said, "Really? Are you sure? You should go look in a mirror." So, I did.

I was shocked to find bright red splotches on my chest and neck, leading right up to my jaw. *Wow*, I had no idea that when I get really nervous, I get splotchy! This was good information for me to learn. Now I know, and I'm aware that still, to this day, if I get nervous, I might get splotchy. If I'm going into a situation where nerves may be an issue, I wear a scarf or shirt with a higher neck coverage as to not give away my nerves to the audience.

Not every fear reaction is visible. How do you know what nerves your audience can see? Take a look at the list of stage fright symptoms shown in Table 3-2.

EXTERNAL	INTERNAL
Flushed face, neck	Nausea
Nervous laughter, smiling	Dry mouth
Increased pace	Increased muscle tension
Ineffective gestures	Increased heart rate
Trembling hands	Butterflies
Monotone	Clavicular breathing
Loss of concentration	Sweaty palms
Low volume	Weak knees
Rambling speech	Blurred vision

Table 3-2. Circle which of these symptoms you experience

If your symptoms fall on the right side of this chart, your audience will never be able to see them; they're all internal reactions. Those on the left side of the list are external, and they can be perceived. Focus on any symptoms you may experience on that side of the list.

When it comes to dealing with those symptoms, don't be afraid to help yourself out! If you find you sweat when you're nervous, make conscious wardrobe choices to help you keep cool. Stay hydrated, and avoid caffeine if you often deal with the shakes. A combination of internal and external work can give you a confident exterior when you take the stage, no matter how you feel inside.

The first few minutes of any presentation can feel the most out of control. Oftentimes, once we get started, we can channel any remaining nerves into the task at hand. Mastery of those first few moments is the key to being a calm and confident presenter.

Franklin D. Roosevelt may have said, "The only thing we have to fear is fear itself," but with effective tools to deal with your stage fright, you won't even have to fear *fear* anymore. You're on your way to more confident and impactful presenting.

Manager's Checklist for Chapter 3

☑ Address why you're nervous. Assess your own feelings of stage fright.

- Make note of team members suffering from a fear of public speaking.
- Find active ways you can help them succeed.

☑ Approach the advance work of your presentation.

- Use the Rehearsal Process to build familiarity and comfort with your presentation.
- Discover a useful personal warm-up to perform in the moments before you go on.

☑ Take the stage with confidence.

- Acknowledge what the audience can see and what they can't.
- Help yourself deal with visible symptoms.
- Create a strong first impression. (See Chapter 9.)

Chapter

4

Audience Analysis

I n my early years as a New York City–based actor, I got a job at the Westchester Broadway Theatre doing a production of *Joseph and the Amazing Technicolor Dreamcoat*. I loved this job. It was three months of singing and dancing to the fun, uplifting music of Andrew Lloyd Webber. It also allowed me to live in my apartment in NYC, versus living out of a suitcase while traveling. We had a company van and drove to the theater, up the West Side Highway, six days a week for three months. I loved my fellow cast members, I loved my small (yet featured) role of Mrs. Potiphar, and I loved that I got to spend a lot of time on a backstage microphone singing high notes.

One day, we were scheduled to do a show for an audience made up exclusively of middle school students. It was an early day for the cast (the show started at 10 a.m.) but, other than that, it was the same show we had done for months—or so we thought. Just a few minutes into the show, something didn't feel right. "What's with them?" we asked each other backstage. "This show feels clunky, everything's off," cast members said. "The audience isn't laughing where they should be, and they're laughing at things that aren't funny." We made it through the two-hour show but complained the whole time. We all felt pretty disappointed when it was over.

In retrospect, the audience wasn't that bad. For middle schoolers, they did pretty well. The ultimate problem: none of us thought about the audience before we took the stage. We just showed up to do our job. Of course they didn't laugh where we normally heard adult audiences laugh. Of course they laughed in places we didn't anticipate. They were middle schoolers! Had we taken a few moments to analyze our audience prior to the start of the show, our expectations would have been different.

Audience Analysis is imperative in business presentations. Here's a series of questions to run through during your content creation process to ensure that you think about all the "what ifs" of your audience.

Audience Demographics

Audiences are fluid.

Even in your standard weekly meeting, people come and go. You see them at a different time or in a different place, which can impact their mental state. Audience members may have experienced organizational changes or changes of heart about an issue that's important to them. Beware of getting used to one particular audience. When it changes, your presentation needs to be adjusted accordingly.

How do you analyze this ever-shifting group? There are two approaches:

1. Sometimes, you'll need to use a bit of imagination and put yourself in the shoes of your listeners. If you know enough about your audience already, you can imagine how they feel about your presentation topic.
2. Other times, you'll need concrete information. Ask the meeting planner, speaker manager, or coordinator connected to your presentation what he or she can tell you about the audience as it relates to your topic.

We'll offer suggestions that use both approaches in the questions that follow.

What Do You Know About Your Audience?

Knowing about the interests and concerns of your audience members allows you to tailor your message to address their needs. Are they knowledgeable about your topic? Is there insider jargon that needs defining or acronyms that may be unfamiliar? Do they already have opinions that you'll need to change before you get them to act? Customize your presentation to talk to your specific audience. One size doesn't fit all.

What's the Win-Win for Your Audience Members?

Finding "what's in it for them" is essential to your success. Address the interests of your audience in your presentation, and illustrate outcomes that yield an improved future for each of them. How can you position your message so that you represent your audience's perspective while assuring them that they're included in your vision of what's to come? Create your presentation so that benefits are clear.

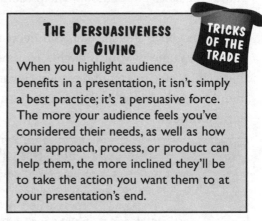

THE PERSUASIVENESS OF GIVING

When you highlight audience benefits in a presentation, it isn't simply a best practice; it's a persuasive force. The more your audience feels you've considered their needs, as well as how your approach, process, or product can help them, the more inclined they'll be to take the action you want them to at your presentation's end.

TRICKS OF THE TRADE

Are There Any Subgroups in Your Audience?

Chances are that any big audience is made up of lots of little audiences. These subgroups may include organizational rank, department, role, tenure, generation, gender, or other distinguishing factors. Is any particular subgroup likely to react to your message differently than the main audience? Does any subgroup have unique needs or fears? Create your presentation to address the concerns of subgroups, while maintaining a message that's true to the audience at large.

Will There Be Outsiders in the Room?

Occasionally, members of other departments, consultants from other firms, or even members of the public may infiltrate your core audience. For those outside your core audience, beware of using local jargon and acronyms that may not be understood. If you choose to use them, you must define them.

Audience Mindset

Have you ever had to sit through a presentation on a topic you don't care about? Conversely, have you ever listened to a presentation on a topic that deeply interests you?

In each situation, your mindset influenced how you received the speaker's message. Good or bad, your state of mind affected your opinion of that speaker's presentation. The presenter didn't stand a chance. Or did she?

When you're the speaker, you need to get "into the shoes" of your audience. Some of your thoughts may be guesses or assumptions, and that's OK. You're not a mind reader! However, considering your audience members' mindset will help you discern the best- and worst-case scenario for them.

ONE LONE VOICE DOESN'T SPEAK FOR THE GROUP

It can be easy to be swayed when you've got an unhappy face in the crowd. But just because one person might not be into what you're saying, don't assume that no one is! One person in your field of vision, or someone with a loud mouth, doesn't necessarily represent the group at large. It's a mistake to cater to only one person's mindset in your presentation.

What's Your Credibility with This Audience?

Your reputation may be positive, negative, or neutral. Does this audience already know you in a positive way? Do you have a history that you need to overcome? Present yourself as qualified and knowledgeable about your topic with a well-crafted introduction. (We'll cover how to introduce yourself in Chapter 6.)

What Preconceived Opinions Might Audience Members Have About Your Content?

Are you walking into a room where the majority of the audience supports your planned message? Or will you need to work a little harder to change their minds? You'll want to be objective but acknowledge contesting viewpoints.

Will There Be an Elephant in the Room?

Sometimes you've been asked to present on a topic that would normally be of interest to your audience, but extenuating circumstances overshadow your presentation. What is going on in the company, in the city, or in the world that may weigh heavily on the minds of your audience at the time of your presentation? What's on your audience members' minds as they arrive for your presentation? Might you strengthen your message by referring to external current events? Last month's presentation may need updating for today's delivery.

Are You Following an "Animal Act"?

Actors are very mindful of who—or what—precedes them on stage. Transitions from one scene or song to another can be abrupt and pose barriers to regaining audience attention. You can't change what a previous speaker says or does, but you can leverage that speaker's message or tone to build a bridge to your presentation. As you build your presentation, keep your mind on what comes before you—whether it's a speaker, a lunch break, a difficult commute, or any sort of disruption that might delay the beginning of your own presentation.

Is Your Presentation Controversial?

As the saying goes, "You can please some of the people all of the time, you can please all of the people some of the time, but you can't please all of the people all of the time." Will there be more than one side to the story you tell in your presentation? Acknowledge both sides. Will some people have their heels dug in, opposing your recommendation? Acknowledge them, too. Create your presentation so that you are informed and thoughtful about all angles, then drive home your message with your own strong rationale.

COURTING CONTROVERSY

Some people just love to keep it edgy. It's part of their personal style to rile, stun, or challenge the room with hot topics and strong language. Remember, this isn't for everyone and can easily backfire. Don't make the mistake of using inflammatory language or humor because you think the whole audience thinks like you. Controversy for the sake of controversy is merely meaningless pot-stirring. You won't risk hurting your message if you keep things professional.

Expectations

Examine your expectations for the audience. Here are two questions you should ask.

1. **What Questions Could You Possibly Get from Your Audience?** Brainstorm the questions you might get, and research the answers. The more you can imagine your audience questions, the less likely you'll be unprepared to answer them. (I'll discuss more about answering questions in Chapter 11.)

2. **Will Anyone Require More Information Than Provided in Your Presentation?** Think about the experts in your audience who'll have more questions than covered in your presentation. Think about the subgroup that's most impacted by the changes you propose. Think about the other managers who need to explain your presentation to their staff or clients. Create your presentation in a way that offers more information to special interest groups later. Consider the needs that go beyond what's covered in your prepared presentation, and cover them in an appendix or in some other form on an as-requested basis.

Audience Analysis Is Essential to Creating Your Presentation

As a presenter, before you think about developing your content, visuals, or supporting materials, you *must* consider your audience. Without your audience, there's no communication taking place. The contents of this chapter may seem like a lot to consider, but don't worry. As you prepare to create your presentation, gather information and build awareness about your audience. The more you consider your audience, the more successful your presentation will be. Use this Audience Analysis list to get closer to your presentation attendees. Be as specific as you can in answering the questions.

> **Audience Demographics**
> 1. What do you know about your audience?
> 2. What's the win-win for your audience members?
> 3. Are there any subgroups in your audience?

4. Will there be outsiders in the room?

Audience Mindset

5. What's your credibility with this audience?
6. What preconceived opinions might audience members have about your content?
7. Will there be an elephant in the room?
8. Are you following an "animal act"?
9. Is your presentation controversial?

Expectations

10. What questions could you possibly get from your audience?
11. Will anyone require more information than provided in your presentation?

Manager's Checklist for Chapter 4

☑ Outline the demographics.

- Ask event planners or managers for any specific information they can give in regard to who will be present.
- Clearly articulate—for your own sake as well as that of your audience—how your presentation will benefit your listeners.
- Be prepared to manage subgroups or unknown attendees.

☑ Get "into the shoes" of your audience, and think about their mindset.

- Discover how you'll deal with those who may disagree or be disinterested in your topic.
- Know what will precede your presentation or if any current events may influence its reception.
- Confront any controversy that your topic may create by acknowledging all points of view.

☑ Manage audience expectations from the outset.

- Brainstorm potential audience questions.
- Create a plan for follow-up, including any extra information or materials audience members may need.

Chapter 5

Acting Techniques That Help You Create Content

When on stage, an actor's job is to change another person's perspective. He or she tries to get someone to do something and, hopefully, feel something. This objective may be focused on a scene partner or the audience at large. A successful combination of a good script and an effective performance causes change. Without change, there's no point to any play.

In business presentations, the goal is the same. You inform an audience so that they react to your message and somehow change their perspective. If you're successful, they react the way you want them to. In this chapter, we'll introduce you to the tools you need to help you discover the overall goal of your presentation and how you will achieve it.

Identifying Your Presentation Objectives

You want your audience to *do* something with the information you give them. Without a clear mission, there's no reason for your presentation.

Identifying your presentation superobjective is the first step toward creating your content. Where do you start? Begin by answering this question:

"When my presentation is over, what's the main thing that I want my audience to do?"

KEY TERMS

Superobjective The primary goal of your presentation. Your superobjective identifies what you want your audience to do after they hear and understand what you have to say.

Objective Smaller, secondary goals embedded in your presentation that align with your superobjective.

The answer to this question is your superobjective.

Using Presentation Strategies

Tactics are steps actors take to get what they want—how they will achieve their objectives. These steps are actions and best described using verbs, such as: to excite, to plead, to warn, to encourage. Tactics can also take the form of humor (to joke) and unique experiences (to share a personal story).

TOOLS

DECONSTRUCT YOUR MOST RECENT PRESENTATION

Think back to your last presentation.

Identify your superobjective, what you wanted your audience to do as a result of your presentation. (It could be something like: "My superobjective was to get my audience to embrace an impending leadership change.)

Superobjective: _____

Identify three objectives that you needed to achieve. It may help to think about the key points in your presentation and what your goal was for each key point. (Something like: "In this section I wanted to introduce the new leader. In the next section, I wanted to put the employees at ease. Finally, I wanted to convince them this is a welcome change.")

Objective 1: _____

Objective 2: _____

Objective 3: _____

KEY TERM

Tactic The means used to achieve a result; your actions to reach your objectives and ultimately achieve your superobjective.

Actors choose their tactics based on the objectives they have planned for their character. Do the same with your presentation. Each objective has a set of tactics to go with it.

Feelings, Nothing More Than...

We can't discuss presentation skills without talking about feelings. Many presenters feel this should be the main focus of their efforts. They think, "I want my audience to feel happy!" or "I want them to love my work." When it comes to feelings, actors know a big secret: you can't make another person feel something.

So, do we just throw feelings out the window? Absolutely not. As a presenter, the way to forge emotional connection, to hopefully help your audience have "feelings" about what you're telling them, is to be clear about what you, as the presenter, are doing. It may sound a bit heady, but there's a big difference between trying to excite someone and trying to make someone "feel" excited. One is forward moving and goal oriented; the other is simply working for an effect. This difficult idea will become clearer throughout this book.

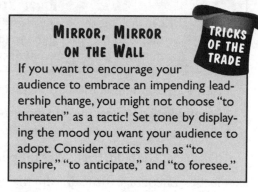

MIRROR, MIRROR ON THE WALL

TRICKS OF THE TRADE

If you want to encourage your audience to embrace an impending leadership change, you might not choose "to threaten" as a tactic! Set tone by displaying the mood you want your audience to adopt. Consider tactics such as "to inspire," "to anticipate," and "to foresee."

Tactics are how you achieve your presentation strategies. They help you put action words to your content so you can attain your superobjective.

Here's a superobjective example: Get the team to embrace a leadership change.

Let's zoom in on one of the objectives:

Objective: Introduce the new leader.

Tactics: Defend the decision to make the change.

Outline how this will be a positive change.

Having trouble identifying tactics? Take another note from the acting world and find obstacles. Obstacles to your presentation are the people, things, or events standing in the way of you achieving your objectives. As a presenter, when you identify what is standing in the way of your communication, you can better choose which tactics are needed to deal with it.

TAKE ANOTHER LOOK

Pick one of your objectives from the previous tool.

Objective: _____

TOOLS   Choose two tactics to go with it. Step back and ask yourself, "What are the steps I can take to achieve this objective?" Remember to use action words!

Tactic 1: _____

Tactic 2: _____

FIRST STEPS FIRST

CAUTION   Keep in mind, this is all prework to creating your presentation content. You're building the road map of big ideas for yourself before you get into the nitty-gritty of the actual words.

Here's an example of these three pieces in action:

Superobjective: To get my audience to embrace an impending leadership change.

(Obstacle: The team really likes the current CEO.)

Tactics: Encourage the team with the new leader's past performance. Connect with them by praising the old leader.

Objective: Introduce the new leader.

(Obstacle: Team fears losing their job with this change.)

Tactics: Calm their fears with information.

You've now identified and articulated your superobjective, objectives, and tactics. We're ready to begin content development in the next chapter.

Manager's Checklist for Chapter 5

☑ Identify your superobjective and objectives.

☑ Identify known and potential obstacles:

- Anticipate specific questios from your audience.
- Identify environmental changes that may occur between planning and presentation delivery.

☑ Identify at least two tactics per objective.

Chapter 6

The Blueprint for Every Presentation

We've identified our objectives and tactics and done our Audience Analysis. Armed with all of our prework, it's time, with the help of this chapter, to put our content together via the Blueprint. Then, we'll translate it into presentation notes that work for you.

The Blueprint is a simple way to put your content together and organize all of your prework (Figures 6-1 through 6-3).

These three pages are the basis of the Blueprint. You can find a full version of the Blueprint in the Appendix.

Introduction

Let's first examine the the introduction to your presentation.

Finding the Perfect Attention Grabber

When I was in college, along with getting my BFA in musical theater, I minored in music education. In one of my education classes, we had to teach a basic musical concept. I was assigned the sixteenth note: what it is and what it does. This mock lesson was intended for elementary school kids, but we were going to deliver it to our college peers. I wanted to teach the most engaging lesson that I possibly could.

I worked out my lesson plan, but I needed to figure out how to put it

INTRODUCTION

	EXTERNAL
Attention Grabber	
You	
Superobjective	
Agenda	
Expectations	

Figure 6-1. Presentation Blueprint: Introduction

SMART

MANAGING

Yours, Mine, and Ours

It's difficult enough when you have your own presentations to plan and deliver. But what if you also need to oversee presentations given by your team for a conference or major event? The Blueprint is an extremely useful tool to implement teamwide. Not only will it help your team develop their presentations (just as it will for you!), but it will help everyone identify problems and make improvements with ease through uniformity of structure. It's far simpler to work on a large project like a major presentation when everyone is speaking the same language conceptually.

---

in the world of my audience—in this case, the college student. So, I based my entire lesson around pizza. I began by asking the class, "Who likes pizza?" After receiving a resounding "Me!" from most of the audience, I presented one very large, whole cheese pizza from my favorite pizza place near campus.

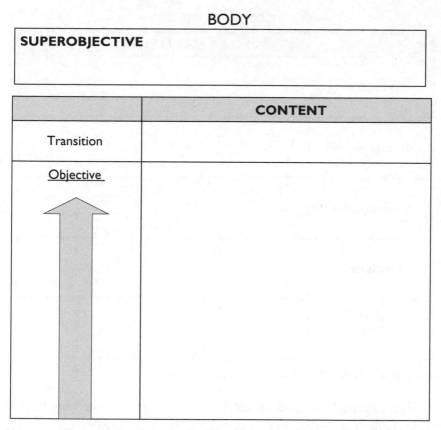

Figure 6-2. Presentation Blueprint: Body

I said, "This pizza is a whole note. If you cut it in half," which I proceeded to do, "you get two half-notes. Cut them in half, you have quarter notes. One more cut, and you have eighth notes." My final cut produced what represented sixteenth notes, and everyone got a small slice of pizza.

I remember glancing at my professor in the back of the room during my lesson. He was furiously taking notes and looking slightly confused. When I got my grade, I was stunned by the first comment the professor wrote: "What the heck are you doing?" (This isn't what he actually wrote but a very cleaned-up version.) The comment that followed was, "Oh, I get it."

He eventually got on board with my lesson plan, but what had inspired his initial response was my attention grabber. Like any good

CONCLUSION

	CONTENT
Transition	
Restate Agenda	
Superobjective	
Appreciation	
Button	

Figure 6-3. Presentation Blueprint: Conclusion

speaker, I wanted my opening statement to say or do something to grab my audience's attention, so I began by asking, "Who likes pizza?"

Pizza has nothing to do with music, and asking about it was unexpected. I had fully grabbed the class's attention. (I also received an A on the assignment with this final comment: "You'd make a great teacher!")

Bear in mind, your attention grabber doesn't have to be cheesy (no pizza pun intended) or awkward, but it should be engaging and perhaps even fun for your audience. Most of all, it should signal that your presentation is about to begin and that you're now in charge of the room.

 Attention Grabber One of the most important parts of your presentation. **KEY TERM** It will make or break the impression the audience has of you. It's the very first thing you say or do at the beginning of your presentation. It lets your audience know your "show" has started.

Where can you begin? Attention grabbers come from a wide variety of sources. They can be simple or elaborate. They can be funny or not. They can be verbal or physical. The possibilities are endless! But whatever you choose, make sure to commit to it fully.

When exploring your attention grabber, try different options. See what feels best to you in your Rehearsal Process. Ask for feedback from peers.

TO WRITE OR NOT TO WRITE? — TRICKS OF THE TRADE

Dedicate time to creating your attention grabber. I recommend mapping out your content first and then returning to the top to solidify your attention grabber. If you're comfortable with thinking on your feet, you can wait until just before your presentation and pull something from your presentation environment. However, if you choose to try an on-the-spot attention grabber, be prepared with a backup in case nothing occurs to you.

ATTENTION GRABBER SUGGESTIONS

TOOLS

- Ask a question of your audience. Make sure you leave time for hands to be raised or an audible response.
- Tell a story (see Chapter 7).
- Display a visual: picture or video.
- Play an audible: music, song, or sound cue.
- Share a quote: lyrics, passage from literature, inspiring words.
- A combination of any or all of the above.

For instance, you might show a picture of someone and ask, "Does anyone know who this is?" This is a unique way to get your audience to look away from their handheld devices and get ready for your presentation!

What if your attention grabber fails? (It happens to all of us: I thought it would be a great idea to make a joke about a member of the New Eng-

ON-THE-SPOT ATTENTION GRABBER — FOR EXAMPLE

I was speaking at an off-site conference and was invited to have lunch with my audience just before I was speaking. One of the women sitting at my table was telling me how much she was enjoying the event. In the most charming singsong voice she said, "This is the best conference everrrrr!"

When I began my presentation I started by saying, "You all have big shoes to fill. Bridget over here just told me that 'This is the best conference everrrr!'"

land Patriots to a Boston-based audience. No one laughed.) If it tanks, don't stress. You've got a lot of time to recover during your presentation. This is why we've also got to have a strong, rehearsed conclusion.

You

It's time to introduce yourself. The most important thing to do is let the audience know who you are and why they should listen to you speak. While you don't need to recite your entire resume or educational history, you should present the audience with the top reasons why you're standing in front of them (Figure 6-4).

You	Director of Marketing, studying trends for 20+ years, avid fan of all social media

Figure 6-4. An example of a three-point "you" introduction

POWER OF THREES

TOOLS In need of a formula for your personal introduction? Share three facts about yourself. Why three? The Three Stooges. The Three Bears. Three Little Maids from School. We inherently love groupings of three. But it's not just because we've heard or seen them since story time in nursery school. Three items are the least number of things you need to make a pattern, and patterns are satisfying to your audience. You'll help them remember who you are long after your presentation is done.

However you choose to introduce yourself, keep it positive. Your introduction sets the tone for the rest of your presentation.

Superobjective

Your next step is to articulate your superobjective to your audience. It's a good thing you already know what that is!

Articulating your superobjective for the audience lets them know what they're in for and what the end goal is. There's absolutely no ambiguity. You'll have a higher likelihood of achieving your goal if you're able to articulate it at the beginning (Figure 6-5).

Agenda

A terrific way to pique the interest of your audience is to let them know what you'll be covering in your presentation. Mind you, you don't need to

Superobjective	My goal is for you to leave here today with tangible tips you can use right away.

Figure 6-5. A concisely communicated super-objective

issue a spoiler alert—there's no need to give away every single topic you're going to address. You may want to keep some elements of your presentation a surprise! But when you give your audience a look at what's coming up, you'll get them on the hook with information they (hopefully!) can't wait to know. Outline your agenda, and you'll help maintain their attention throughout the presentation (Figure 6-6).

Expectations

Agenda	Presentation basics, storytelling, the inevitable stage fright

Figure 6-6. A brief highlight of an agenda

This final part of the introduction is your chance to set the rules for your presentation. This is the time to let your audience know if you want to take questions during the presentation or at the end during a Q&A portion. (We'll address the different ways of handling Q&A later.) Audience expectations might also include breaks you'll take during your session, logistics you want to announce (like the location of beverages or restrooms), or physical activity involved in the session (perhaps for interactive exercises). Remember, this is your show, and this is your time to set the rules (Figure 6-7).

Expectations	3-hour session, two 15-minute breaks

Figure 6-7. An outline of some expectations

Organizing Your Presentation Body

The body pages are the place to organize all of your content outside of the introduction and conclusion. You can use as many of these pages as needed (See the Blueprint in the Appendix.)

At the top of each page, you'll notate your superobjective. That doesn't change. We leave it there as a constant reminder, to keep it top-of-mind. All of your content always works toward your superobjective.

You want to dedicate one page to each individual objective. Remember, these are different than your superobjective, and usually align nicely with your key points.

Transition

There's a line on the body page for a transition. As with our attention grabber, they can be as simple or elaborate as you'd like, as long as they signal to the audience that you're moving on to another major thought. You're helping the audience follow you from one section to another, or from one thought to the next (Figure 6-8).

Transition	Let's get started.

Figure 6-8. An example of a good transition

Objectives and Tactics

The left column is used to list each of your individual objectives and the tactics you will use to achieve each goal. On the right side you can list some thoughts, or perhaps even the actual words, that you may want to use during your presentation. Don't forget, one body page=one objective. However, you'll likely have multiple tactics per objective (Figure 6-9).

Say you've chosen three tactics for a particular objective. They are to warn your audience of impending doom, to prepare them for a rocky road, and to comfort them with a potential positive outcome. When you're developing your content, you can link up those tactics with your notes, as in Figure 6-9.

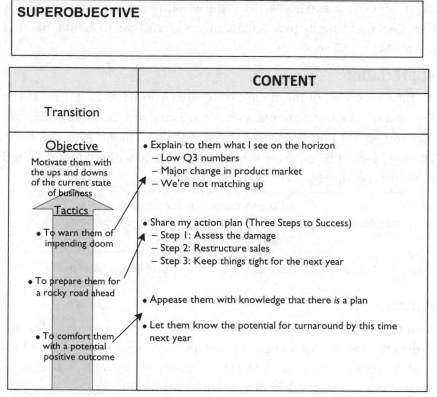

Figure 6-9. Sample body page with objectives and tactics

Conclusion

Finally we come to the end of the presentation. Here's how to do this effectively.

Restate Your Agenda

Now, we simply need to remind the audience of what they've heard and give one last push toward your superobjective. With one last transition, you'll move to restating your agenda (Figure 6-10).

Restate Agenda	Essential presentation skills, storytelling, foolproof ways to get rid of your stage fright

Figure 6-10. Restate your agenda

Superobjective

Don't forget, your superobjective is the whole reason you're there! This is your final opportunity to articulate this powerful call to action. Remind them what it's all about.

Appreciation

It's time to say all of the "thank yous" that you need to (Figure 6-11). Thank any meeting planners, VIPs, or players within the organization that you want to acknowledge. Most important, thank your audience. They've been with you every step of the way, and without them, there'd be no presentation!

Appreciation	I'd like to thank Eric for scheduling this presentation as well as all of you for being a fantastic audience.

Figure 6-11. Thank those you need to in the appreciation section

Button

In musical terms, the button of a song is the very last moment of music at the end that lets the audience know it's time to applaud. It might be a loud chord, or a drum roll, or a cymbal crash. Whatever it is, it inspires the audience to respond, hopefully with rousing cheers!

In terms of a business presentation, the button is your opportunity, as the presenter, to do the same. The button is the flip side of your attention grabber: you use the attenion grabber to let the audience know it's time to begin, and the button to let the audience know it's time to end. Give your button as much care as you did your attention grabber! It might be a story, a quote, or even a reiteraion of your superobjective. Remember, the button is the very last thing your audience will hear, so be sure to make it memorable.

Working with Your Performance Notes

Your content is now all mapped. Prior to beginning your Rehearsal Process, you need to put together your presentation notes. What your notes look like is completely up to you; there are many different options and styles. Try a few of them during your Rehearsal Process to see which

---

Button It Up!

Try some of these:

- A song quote that relates to your point: "As the great Rolling Stones once said, 'You can't always get what you want.' But clearly right now, we're getting what we need."
- A story about your presentation experience, with a restatement of your superobjective: "On the way here this morning, I was thrilled about sharing these findings with you. I hope you are as pleased as I am and inspired to go out and tell your patients the good news."
- Echo your attention grabber: "I've enjoyed my time here today; it certainly is 'The best conference everrrrrr.'"

---

makes the most sense for you.

When writing out your notes, work toward short bullets or an outline of ideas. You'll be well rehearsed for the actual presentation, so your notes are just a few words to prompt you in the right direction. Some speakers will highlight a few of the most important words of their presentation in their bulleted notes.

Types of Presentation Notes

As mentioned, there are lots of different ways to take and use your presentation notes. It's all about what works for you. Here are a few ideas to get you started:

Use the Blueprint

Visual Creation

Once your Blueprint is completed, it is now the ideal time to create your visuals. Let them be informed by your Blueprint, superobjective, objectives, and tactics. Bear in mind, if your visuals are already created, you *still* need to do this prework. Visuals aren't a substitute for the Blueprint.

Size Matters

Whether your notes are a hard copy, digital, or viewable on a confidence monitor along with your visuals, make sure the font size works for you. It's very frustrating as an audience member to watch a speaker struggle with reading glasses or excessive squinting when referring to his or her notes. Also, make sure that if you're working from paper, your pages are numbered sequentially. If possible, staple them together.

The Blueprint as a whole allows you to keep track of where you are in your presentation and helps you keep an eye on your objectives and tactics. A simplified option is to use only the content side of the Blueprint (the right side of the individual body pages) as your performance notes (see Figure 6-9).

Notes-to-Visuals

To ensure your content is matching up with your visuals, print out a small version of each slide or visual with your corresponding notes.

Visuals Only

If you don't want to hold paper or a device, opt for entering your performance notes into the visual program itself. This can be especially helpful when speaking in large conference rooms or theaters. Often, there will be a monitor placed in front of you, out of sight of the audience. With a quick glance, you can stay on track and on point.

CAUTION

LEAVE MEMORIZATION TO THE ACTORS

Writing out your script can be a very helpful technique. However, you shouldn't memorize an entire script for your presentation. You can memorize elements of your presentation (the introduction and conclusion are good options), but it can be detrimental to your delivery to rely on memory for your entire presentation. What happens if you forget your next line?

Without professional training, a recited script can sound just like that—a recited script. The goal here is to get your audience to change their perspective and take action. To do that well, you need to create an emotional connection with your listeners. If the audience thinks you're reading, even if it's just reading a script from your brain, the authentic connection is difficult to achieve. Just say no to script memorization.

Following is a sample of my notes from an actual presentation (Figure 6-12). I like simple phrases. I use an asterisk to identify where my visuals change and a B where I black out the screen completely. (We'll address this in Chapter 8.) I always have the superobjective on top as a constant reminder of my overall goal.

The Blueprint takes the guesswork out of presentation prep. Just as a builder wouldn't dream of starting a new house without a plan, you shouldn't think about giving a presentation without one!

BODY

SUPEROBJECTIVE
To excite audience to use new skills right away.

	CONTENT
Transition	Moving On to Verbal Viruses ✱

Objective
• educate them on the plague of Verbal Viruses
Tactics
 	
• explain why we defer to "ums"
 	
• demo power of pause
 	
• have them practice on feet
	• Why do we "um"?
	  - Brain moves faster than mouth
	  - we don't like silence ✱
	
	• Solution-Pause
	  - try it in "small bites"
	Ⓑ
	
	• On Your Feet
	  - tell the person next to you what you did in the first 15 minutes of your day today - No Verbal Viruses - PAUSE!

Figure 6-12. Sample of marked performance notes

Manager's Checklist for Chapter 6

☑ Craft your introduction. Don't forget to include:
  ■ An attention grabber to take hold of your listeners.
  ■ A section all about *you*.
  ■ A brief outline of your agenda.
  ■ Expectations for your audience.

☑ Organize your content.
- Make sure your superobjectives and tactics take a front seat!
- Use transitions to keep your audience on track.
- Fill out as many sheets as there are objectives in your presentation.
- Create your conclusion.

☑ Restate your agenda.
- Remind your audience of your superobjective.
- Thank all the necessary parties.
- Put a button on it.

☑ Decide what format you will use for your presentation notes.

Storytelling for Audience Engagement

T ake a moment right now and think back to a year ago. What's the first memory that pops into your mind? What's the first thing you can recall from 12 months ago? My guess is that whatever you remember, it's tied to a strong emotion. It could be good, bad, happy, sad, or any of a million emotions in between. We, as humans, remember emotions first and details second.

As my all-time favorite quote from the great Maya Angelou states: "I've learned that people will forget what you said, people will forget what you did, but people will never forget how you made them feel."

This is why we tell stories. This is why we *need* stories in presentations. If you can weave information into one big story, or tie information forward or back to a story, you'll connect an emotion to it. When there's an emotion surrounding your content, it will be infinitely more memorable to your audience, and they'll be more likely to take your desired action.

If stories connect emotionally (and I 100 percent believe that they do), that in turn immediately builds trust and rapport between you and your listeners and can shake them out of a staid mindset. When you present only data and facts, you keep your audience in "critical thinking" mode. When they're restricted to thinking critically, their mind is more inclined to find ways to push back on, or shut down to, the information that you are giving them. Data and facts are important. Data and facts persuade, but emotion inspires people to take action.

Telling stories is also more enjoyable for everyone involved. Entertainment potential aside, our brains love a story. A satisfying story ending activates our sensory cortex and triggers the limbic system to release dopamine. Similar to the "runner's high," a story can make people feel better. And when your audience is feeling good, they'll be more open to listening to your ideas, your data, or even difficult news.

Effective storytelling is a skill. Simply rambling off a bunch of stories with no previous thought, effort, or relation to your content won't yield the benefits of emotional connection. But, never fear, it's a skill you can learn. This chapter will help you discover how, when, and where to incorporate stories in your presentations to create that all-important emotional bond with your audience.

How to Tell a Story

With all due deference to Aristotle, there's a bit more to storytelling than just a beginning, middle, and end. Any story you tell, be it 30 seconds or 30 minutes long, needs to have six elements: exposition, inciting incident, rising action, climax, falling action, and resolution.

These six plot elements originate with a German playwright and author named Gustav Freytag, who lived in the nineteenth century. He

KEY TERMS **Exposition** Sets the scene for your audience. The opening of your story that tells the audience the who, what, when, and where of the action.

Inciting incident The major event that sparks the action of the story, the event that makes this day different from all other days, the event that changes the normal course of action.

Rising action Comprises the smaller occurrences that lead up to the story's climax. It's the engine that keeps the story moving.

Climax The big moment, the major revelation, the turning point or "ah-ha!" of the story.

Falling action The winding down of the story; the "wrap-up" events that lead to the resolution.

Resolution The answer, solution, moral, or "lessons learned" portion of your story.

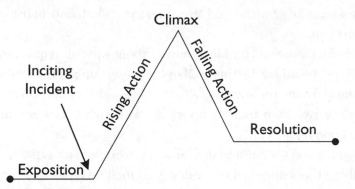

Figure 7-1. The Story Map

created what came to be known as "Freytag's Pyramid": a graphic-based layout of what he discerned to be the most common dramatic story arc. His analysis of the structure of stories was spot-on, and still holds to this day. It can be found in plays, movies, and written stories of any kind. I simply call this the Story Map (Figure 7-1). It's an easy way to navigate the action when creating a story to use during your presentations.

Chances are, you may be familiar with some of these terms. Good! Let me show you a breakdown of how they work in a real-life story. Like all of the stories in this book, this is true and from my life. I'll use this story as our guinea pig and apply parts of it to the Story Map.

Exposition

"One of the many nonactor jobs I had while living in New York City was selling payroll for one of the big national payroll companies. I had a teeny-tiny territory in midtown Manhattan. It was three blocks long and two avenues wide. I spent a lot of time trying to get appointments with business owners and visiting as many small businesses as I could."

This sets the scene of my story. I told you that I was an actor working at a payroll company (who), that I spent a lot of time selling payroll (what), that it was an event from my past (when), and that I lived in New York City (where). The rest of my story will encompass the "why." I included some colorful details to help paint a picture for you, the listener.

Inciting Incident

"One day, I was sitting at the desk in my cube, making some cold calls, when my manager walked over to me with a big stack of papers. Because he knew I was an actor, he said, 'Hey Kerri, you like to talk in front of people don't you?'

"'Yeah?' I answered timidly, guarded about what his request might be.

"'Here!' he said as he threw all of the papers on my desk. 'Tomorrow morning at 9 a.m., there are 20 CPAs coming to this office. You're going to deliver this two-hour training on fringe tax benefits for New York State. Have a good night!'"

My manager's request to deliver this last-minute presentation wasn't something that happened every day. This inciting incident changed my course of action and made this day different from all of the other days that I sat at my desk making phone calls.

Rising Action

"I stared at the stack papers. It was a printout of a PowerPoint deck supporting the material that I needed to deliver. I didn't know much about fringe benefits, but I was confident in my ability as an actor to analyze my 'script' and prepare to deliver a decent training session. So, I began like any good actor would.

"First, I read the deck and the training manual. I nearly fell asleep right there sitting in my cube. 'Wow,' I thought, 'This really needs some help.' I immediately started a talk-through out loud. I found areas of the training where I could tell some personal stories. I made notes on the printout of my PowerPoint deck and then got on my feet for my walk-through. A few hours later, I was ready for my dress rehearsal.

"It was after office hours, so I had the training room all to myself. I stood in the front of the room and I delivered the session just as I would the following morning. I felt pretty good and was ready to go. I packed up my stuff and headed to the subway to go home."

I told you every step I took along the way after my inciting incident. In this story, my rising action elements happened to include the Rehearsal Process! However, I also told you what happened before I started my rehearsal, as well as what happened after.

The Climax

"During my subway ride, I was going over the presentation in my head. Did I have enough stories to tell? Would it be engaging? Were people going to leave with the information they need about fringe benefits?

"And then it hit me. 'What this presentation needs is a costume!' I thought to myself. As soon as I got back to my apartment, I rummaged through my closet and found an old leather jacket with fringe on the sleeves. That was it! That was what would make my presentation memorable! My plan was to show off the fringe on my jacket every time I said 'fringe benefits.'"

The climax of the story, my big "ah-ha moment," was the discovery that my presentation needed a costume. It's the high point of my whole story. Everything that happens from here on out will be the descent to the finish.

Falling Action

"Then, the next morning, in front of 20 New York City CPAs, that's exactly what I did.

"I presented the information at a good pace. I told a few stories that loosely tied back to the concept that I was introducing. I donned my fringed leather jacket over my business suit, and every time I said the phrase 'fringe benefits,' I opened my arms nice and wide so everyone could see the fringe. The audience watched me in a slightly stunned manner, but everyone stayed in the room for the entire two hours. For the duration, I got a lot of nonverbal encouragement; there were a lot of head nods and good eye contact from the audience throughout. I was pleased with my performance."

In this case, the falling action of my story was actually the delivery of the presentation itself. Giving the performance, showing off the fringe, and receiving good feedback are all action elements that lead toward the resolution.

Resolution

"What I was most pleased with was that out of all of the payroll reps that delivered training that day, I was rated the highest. And I thought, 'There is something to this rehearsal preparation and storytelling ...' That was the very first seedling that became my company, Ovation Communication.

"Incidentally, I also learned that training sessions don't need costumes."

My resolution to this story always includes the overall point of the story (that my rehearsal and storytelling efforts made a difference), the lessons I learned (that training sessions don't require a costume—whoops!) and the future action it sparked (the creation of my own company).

When I deliver this story in a presentation skills training session, I'm teaching the audience through my own actions—not only laying out an interesting story according to the Story Map, but tying it back to my content for that day.

You've got plenty of stories from your own life that you can use to do exactly the same thing. I know you do. However, you want to make sure that, regardless of the story you tell, it follows the Story Map. If you're not sure that's the case, Figure 7-2 is a worksheet with questions to help you develop each of the points on the map.

STORY PROMPTS	
Exposition	Who was involved? What was the environment? When was it? Where did it happen?
Inciting Incident	What main event occurred that forced the rest of the action in the story?
Rising Action	What key actions occurred that helped build up the climax? 1. 2. 3. 4.
Climax	What crowning moment occurred that the rising led to?

Figure 7-2. Story prompts to get your story started (continued on next page)

Falling Action	What was the direct result of the climax?
Resolution	What is the purpose or lesson(s) learned?

Figure 7-2. Story prompts to get your story started (concluded)

Incorporating Stories into Presentations

You can use a story or stories at any time during your presentation. There are, however, three specific applications where a story really shines: as an opener or closer, as a vehicle to put facts in context, and woven throughout your presentation. Each option is effective. They can ensure that your storytelling is purposeful and always related to your content.

Using a Story to Open or Close Your Presentation

A powerful place to use a story is right at the top of your presentation, as the attention grabber. Opening with a story lets your audience know they're in for something different. If you launch right into a story (versus the old standby line: "Hi, my name is Kerri and I'm super excited to be here today."), your audience will be pleasantly surprised and ready to listen to you.

Stories that start off your presentation don't have to be long. Depending on how much time you have for your presentation, a 30-second or 1-minute story will suffice. In the case of a starter story, you don't even necessarily need to speak directly to your content. It could be a mode for introducing yourself, or a foreshadowing of what's to come. If you can actually make a connection between your opening story and your content, even better.

You can also use a story to close your presentation as your button. The button is going to solicit a reaction from your audience (hopefully applause) and let them know the presentation is over. It's the last thing they'll hear and might be the piece of information they remember most. A

HIGH-TECH TELLING

FOR EXAMPLE

A few years ago, I was working with a speaker at a high-tech company. She was introducing a new version of an existing accounting system. She began her presentation by telling this story as her attention grabber:

"I just got back from a fabulous theme park vacation in Florida. My husband and I are always excited to take our two kids on these kind of vacations.

"This year, we decided to invest in some fast pass bracelets that would help us speed through lines at the park. But we couldn't figure out how to use them, and we had to get help to activate the bracelets correctly.

"At our first ride, it took a few tries to get it to work. At our second ride, the scanning was much faster. By the time we had lunch, we were all pros at presenting our wrists in the perfect manner for the scanner to read them on the first try. It took a couple of hours and frustrated my children, but the wristbands eventually made the trip much more fun and a lot easier.

"That's what I want to talk about today: using new technology may take some getting used to but ultimately will make your life a lot easier."

This introductory story took about a minute to tell. And while not directly related to her content, we learned a lot about the storyteller. In just one minute, she started to make an emotional connection with her audience. By the end of this story, the audience was ready to listen and knew that the thrust of her presentation would be about new technology that would require a bit of an adjustment.

JUST LAUNCH INTO THE STORY

TRICKS OF THE TRADE

By nature, stories are engaging. You don't need to begin by saying, "Today I'm going to tell you a story about the time I went to a theme park." Just jump into the story and take your audience on an unexpected journey. They'll be intrigued with this opening and you'll have them in the palm of your hand.

closing story will ensure that your all-important emotional connection with your audience remains intact.

Putting Facts into Context

Telling a story at any time gives your audience's brain a nice break from the nitty-gritty, dry content, or heavy data you may be covering. After hearing a story and activating a different part of their brain—even if it's just for a minute—they'll be ready to jump back in and hear about numbers, codes, or any other details that may need to be presented, perhaps even with a better understanding of how they work.

A story can also be used to highlight some key points or put a fact into context. Perhaps a sagging set of sales numbers reminds you of the season when your favorite football team went from winning the Super Bowl to coming in last place in the league. The story of a downturn in production not only comes through but gets "underlined" with this example from another industry.

One of the things I cover when I speak on professional presence is a tip about how to quickly change your own mood. I like to highlight this key point, and put the fact into context, with this story:

"A few years ago, I was spending a training day with a group of eight speakers in Fargo, North Dakota. They were learning essential presentation skills, and I was helping them get ready for an upcoming conference. When lunch break rolled around, all the speakers left to eat, and I had a few quiet minutes in the room alone to check my phone.

"I had a number of missed phone calls and text messages from my husband telling me to call him immediately. I called him back and learned that our dog, a four-pound rescue Maltese, had suddenly passed away. This was a shock to me, and I was extremely sad.

"Unfortunately, I didn't have enough time to get upset. I had a very short lunch break. I was on-site at a client's office, so maintaining my professionalism was extremely important—I didn't want to be known as the trainer who cried.

"I took a few deep core breaths, and I smiled. Initially, I felt ridiculous. I felt sad, and I felt angry. But after just a few seconds of standing there smiling, I started to feel better. I continued to smile, maybe a minute more, and my mood lifted. I was able to get through the second half of the training day without falling apart and breaking down over the loss of my beloved dog."

This story connects with the audience well and puts the tip into context. Many people have, or have had, dogs in their life. If not a dog, then, unfortunately, they've experienced the loss of something (or someone) vitally important at some point. By sharing my story of loss, and how I dealt with some of it in the moment, I'm connecting with their own emotional experiences of the same.

BE A STAR IN YOUR STORY

Some people find it difficult to talk about themselves. They're reluctant to discuss their own experiences or feel that they don't have any stories worth sharing. But the most powerful stories, the ones most likely to make an emotional connection with your audience, will be about you—or at least involve you as a main character. No matter how much you love your buddy Jason's story about the night he partied with Grammy-winning rock stars, it's not going to resonate with your audience the same way that your own story will.

The same goes for client success stories. They can be moving, but make sure you were involved in their success or that it somehow comes back to your experience with it. The story of how your team led a client to record numbers is far more inspiring than the story of how an unrelated team in another state did it. Personal is engaging.

The piece of information that I want to highlight in my presentation is this: smile when you're upset to trick your brain to thinking you're in a better mood. My story not only utilizes that tip, but demonstrates a real-life application. It's one thing just to hear a tip, fact, or step in a process. Tell how it was used in a real-life situation and the audience is more likely to remember the advice you're giving them and take the action that you'd like them to.

Weaving a Story Throughout

Like most of the skills in this book, storytelling is flexible. There are many ways to do it effectively. But perhaps the most flexible application of storytelling is weaving a story throughout your presentation.

Begin your story as your attention grabber. Tell the audience a little bit more about your journey in each of the presentation's transitions. Bring everything together and tell them the story end during the final part of your conclusion.

This adds great energy and interest to your content. It keeps the audience on the hook throughout your presentation, wondering what's going to happen next. Often, the resolution of the story drives home a major takeaway from your content—the life-changing thing about this information. When you weave a story into well-laid-out content, you've got a fully engaged audience.

Storytelling Is Fluid

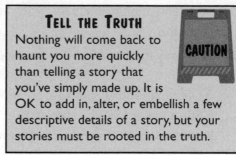

TELL THE TRUTH

Nothing will come back to haunt you more quickly than telling a story that you've simply made up. It is OK to add in, alter, or embellish a few descriptive details of a story, but your stories must be rooted in the truth.

I'm fond of each of these three applications. What's great is that you don't have to use just one of them! Mix them up, combine them, and come up with your own best practices. Tell a story as an attention grabber. Use another to highlight a major point. Weave yet another in and out of your presentation. The choice is yours.

If you're new to storytelling and want to just dip your toe in the water, my best advice is to start with a short story as your attention grabber. This is a great way to test your comfort level with storytelling and gauge your audience's reaction. I suggest trying this at the beginning versus the end because if it doesn't go as smoothly as you'd like, you've still got your entire well-organized, well-rehearsed presentation to make up for it. But, if you use the Story Map and the Story Prompt questions to build your story, and apply the Rehearsal Process to it with as much care and time as you do for the rest of your presentation, you're highly unlikely to deliver anything other than a fantastic, engaging story.

As humans, we love stories. Look at all of the money we spend on movies, music, television, books: we're always looking to hear a great one. Your audience is already waiting to hear something good.

Actors know this secret: a waiting audience is always looking for you to succeed. So, be brave and tell them a story! You'll offer them something really engaging; they'll leave with useful details that they remember because of the emotional connection you've created. They'll connect with the information coming out of your mouth, no matter how dry that information may be.

Manager's Checklist for Chapter 7

☑ Stories create emotional connections. Embrace the idea of storytelling in your presentations!

☑ Build a well-structured story around the points of the Story Map:

exposition, inciting incident, rising action, climax, falling action, and resolution.

☑ Pick a way (or many ways) to incorporate a story into your presentation.

- Openings and closings are great places to tell a story.
- Stories at any point can help put major points in context.
- Stories woven throughout take your audience on a journey.

☑ Tell stories in the way that works for you, but make sure they're detailed, truthful, and *yours*.

Chapter
8

Performance Techniques

There's a famous moment in the musical *A Chorus Line* when the director of the show calls out to one of the dancers, "Don't pop the head, Cassie!" He's trying to tone down the star quality of one of the women auditioning for his show. He wants her to blend in with the chorus, not stand out from the crowd.

Some people just stand out. They're not meant to blend in. However, whether you're a natural showstopper, or your presentation skills need a little polish, there are things you can do that will make the most of what you've got and wow the crowd. That's what this chapter is about: embracing extra techniques that enhance your presentation skills so you can look and feel like a superstar when you're presenting.

Make It All About You

While your content and your superobjective are all about your audience, your performance techniques are all about you. You're the main event! Your job as the presenter is to make it as easy as possible for your audience to hear you, see you, and understand what you're saying.

A surefire way to get your audience to focus on you is to only give them the option to look at one thing—you. That means when you're presenting, and you truly want to connect with your audience, it's best to turn off your visuals.

JUST A HEADS-UP ...

If you're going to black out your screen, you want to inform your audience that you're going to do so. You can simply say, "I like to use the blackout key a lot during my presentations. It looks like this." Then, show them the function in action. This will help you avoid audience confusion. You'll bypass any thoughts that your technology has misfired and let them know any disappearing visuals are intentional.

"Blasphemy!" you may say. How can you possibly survive without something on the screen behind you? You can. In fact, you'll raise the level of direct connection with your audience when you stop asking them to split their focus by looking at you *and* your screen. You can accomplish this by using the blackout function that can be found in many different programs. If you're using a remote to control your visuals, you may even have an individual blackout key available to you. Shutting your visuals off momentarily works in a large room, a small room, or even in a one-on-one conversation. Remember, the goal is to have the audience look at and listen to you, the presenter. It's easier for them to know which of those two things you'd like them to do when you get rid of other visual distractions.

Control Your Visuals

Of course, there are lots of times when you need your visuals to be visible. When you need to share your stage with visuals of any kind, remember: it's your stage and your show. Visuals are there to enhance your performance and make it easy for your audience to understand your message. They shouldn't dominate the presentation. When you want your audience to pay attention to a piece of data, a software function, a video, or other visual, a bit of performance technique can help you effectively share the stage with your supporting technology.

If you want people to look at something on a screen that is behind or to the side of you, start by giving them a specific instruction. Tell them where their eyes should go, and then give the audience time for their eyes to go there. Take a step to the right or left to open yourself up to the screen. This helps your audience continue to see your face while clearing the screen behind you.

Then, *stop talking.*

Allow the audience a moment to see and comprehend the information you're sharing with them before you continue to speak.

Look Where You Want the Audience to Look

A lot of time is spent in the theater getting the audience

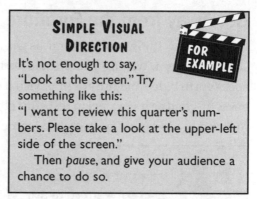

SIMPLE VISUAL DIRECTION

It's not enough to say, "Look at the screen." Try something like this:

"I want to review this quarter's numbers. Please take a look at the upper-left side of the screen."

Then *pause*, and give your audience a chance to do so.

to look at exactly the right place at the right time, to catch the piece of action the director wants them to. The director may accomplish this through a variety of technical means (spotlights, etc.). But perhaps the strongest directional option available on stage is the focus of the other actors. The audience looks where the actors look, so a director will ensure that all of the actors are looking in the same place for certain important moments.

Your own gaze is just as powerful a tool in your presentation. To get your audience to look where you want them to look, you, the presenter, need to look there yourself. Want the audience to focus on your screen? Turn (momentarily) and look at it yourself. Want them to focus on a flipchart or small item in your hand? Same thing. Always use your visual focus to guide that of the audience. (We'll cover this technique in Chapter 10.)

AVOID VISUAL TEMPTATION

One thing that has tempted many presenters is the siren song of their own visuals. Whether as a nervous reaction, or an act of subconscious admiration, lots of speakers find themselves sucked in to staring at, and speaking almost exclusively to, their screens or other visuals.

When you turn and look at your visuals in an effort to guide audience focus, be sure to return to facing front before you begin speaking again. It might feel good to just keep staring at that screen and pretend your audience isn't there. But you'll never connect with your listeners if you spend an entire hour speaking to everything but your audience.

Get Away from the Furniture

If there's one thing I can't stand as an audience member, it's the old standby lectern. Why do I loathe a lectern? Because it's an invitation for speakers to hide a majority of their visual communication from the audience. As good as it may feel to rest your elbows on a lectern, if you choose to stand behind one, you merely become a talking head.

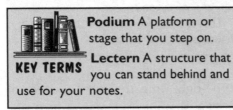

Podium A platform or stage that you step on.

Lectern A structure that you can stand behind and use for your notes.

KEY TERMS

There's a difference between a podium and a lectern—and an easy way to remember it. The word *podium* comes from the Latin root *ped*, or *pod* in Greek. Both *ped* and *pod* reference the foot. (Think *podiatrist*—the foot doctor.) So, a podium is something you put your feet on.

Lectern comes from the same Latin root as the word *lecture*. And from where are many lectures delivered? That's right, a lectern. This is because, often, lecturers want a place to rest their notes. To recap: *lectern*, where speakers stand and rest their notes during a "lecture." *Podium*, where speakers stand and rest their "pods"—errrr, feet—for a presentation.

Regardless of your height, lecterns can hide a large portion of your body from your audience. Since we know that your physicality is a huge part of the overall communication of your message, taking that much of your body out of commission is a detriment to you. The best thing you can do? Step away from the lectern. Let your audience see your entire body. Use strong gestures and stage movement to your advantage. Even if you need to stand next to the lectern in order to stay "in your light," it's still better for your audience than standing behind it. (We'll talk about "finding your light" in Chapter 9.)

You may find yourself in a situation where your microphone is attached to the lectern. If that happens, see if you can point the microphone toward one side of the lectern or the other so that you're still able to stand next to it rather than behind it (Figure 8-1). Most lecterns have moveable microphones.

Remember, it's your stage. Should you arrive for a presentation and a lectern is present, be brave and see if you can have it removed. Your audi-

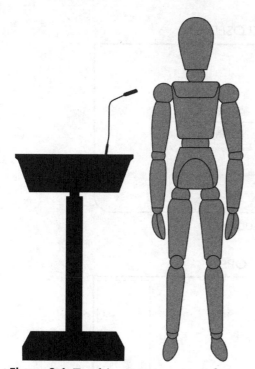

Figure 8-1. Try this setup to get out from behind the lectern

ence will thank you. If you can't have it taken away, you're now armed with solutions to avoid the fate of a talking head.

What about when you *need* to use the furniture on stage? The same still holds true: avoid standing behind it as much as possible. Here's a way to make your presentation space more presenter (and audience) friendly. Take a look at the stage layout in Figure 8-2.

You'll notice that the demo table, computer and all, has been positioned in such a way that you can run your demo while facing your audience and still have an open space in which to present—eureka! Any time you don't have to use your computer, you can step away from the table entirely, take center stage, and use strong movement to really connect with your listeners. No hiding behind tables for you!

If you're in a situation where you can't move your table, you should still embrace the idea of stepping out from behind it and getting closer to the audience whenever you can. Want a double dose of power? Present what you need to from your computer, then black out your screen and cross in front of your table, closer to your audience. You'll have complete command of your presentation space.

Don't Match the Backdrop

If you're unfamiliar with the location of your speaking engagement, ask the meeting planner, or anybody else who may know, what color the backdrop will be when you are speaking.

CLOSED

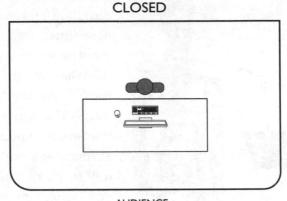

AUDIENCE

OPEN

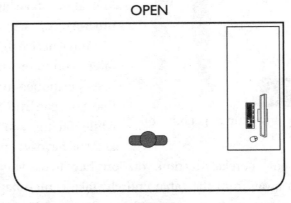

AUDIENCE

Figure 8-2. Bird's-eye view of an adjusted stage layout

KEY TERM **Backdrop** The hanging behind you when you're on stage. It's often used to cover lighting instruments, or stage infrastructure, or simply to give presenters (and actors) a clean "set" to stand in front of. Backdrops are often made of stage curtain material; however, they may also be a screen or a tarp-like material branded with the logos of various sponsors or products.

The goal of this entire chapter is to make you stand out and not blend in. Despite all of your best efforts, if you visually fade away into the background, you'll fall short of your goal!

The key to standing out from your backdrop is in wardrobe color selection. You want

> ### Strong, Bold Color
>
> **TRICKS OF THE TRADE**
>
> Stage actors spend a lot of time performing in front of large, black curtains, or in small stage spaces called "black boxes." In a black box, *everything* in the space is black—walls, floor, ceiling, everything. In most cases, a costume designer gets to worry about this problem. However, occasionally, the actors may be dressing themselves. Many actors choose to wear jewel tones on stage for just this reason: emerald greens, ruby reds, subtle golds, and deep purples can keep them from visually fading away. Wearing a suit? Navy with a white shirt and a bold tie can do the trick as well.

to choose a color that contrasts with your backdrop to avoid "floating-head syndrome." This will also help your audience see you if the lighting is dim. If you can't get this information ahead of time, bring a few different top options to your speaking engagement, and try to find out your backdrop color ASAP.

Reading Your Audience

Reading your audience can be difficult. If you're on a big stage, it's hard to see the looks on people's faces or what their body language is saying. Remember, Audience Analysis always helps. (If you haven't already, go back and review Chapter 4.)

If you're close enough to actually see your audience, like in a small conference room, look for positive verbal and nonverbal cues to see if they're with you. Head nods and smiles are obviously a good sign, as is more looking up at you than down at devices. (Bear in mind that this isn't a hard-and-fast rule. Personally, I've been very engaged in certain presentations but chosen to take notes on a device. I try to remember this when I have audience members buried in their devices.)

An obvious, but often overlooked, technique is the audience check-in. To easily see if they're engaged, simply ask them! Be sure to wait for an actual response—whether a head nod, raised hand, or verbal answer—from your audience before moving on.

Meeting and Greeting

If you have the opportunity, take a few minutes prior to your presentation to meet and greet your audience. You'll get a good feel for what's going on with them if you simply talk to them.

SMART

MANAGING

AUDIENCE ENGAGEMENT CHECK-IN

As a manager, it's important to know that your team is with you. You're going to need them to take action on your information at some point—otherwise, why give a presentation at all? A simple audience check-in is effective regardless of whether you're presenting to your team, your entire organization, or people you've never met at a conference. Want to make sure that your audience is with you? Try these:

"Any questions up to this point?"
"Are you with me?"
"Does this make sense so far?"
"Sound good?"

When I don't know my audience, I work hard to introduce myself to as many people as possible beforehand, regardless of the size of the crowd. I ask, "What are you hoping to get out of today's session?" This informal poll doesn't alter my content—that's already set and well rehearsed—but it allows me to hone in on points that may be hot topics for the audience. Also, the more people I meet, the more names and personal references I can use during my presentation.

Meeting and greeting your audience arms you with more information, while helping you build a rapport with them. This simple action shows that you care about your listeners and their needs and concerns. They'll be more inclined to listen to you because you've shown interest in them before you've even begun your presentation.

REFERENCE YOUR MEET AND GREET

FOR EXAMPLE

When you make the effort to meet and greet your audience, you can add personalized statements like this to your presentation:

"I was speaking to Marvin from accounting prior to this presentation, and he's really interested in top tips for presentation nerves. Anyone else looking for similar advice?"

Here are some other meet-and-greet questions you can ask your audience as they arrive:

"What brings you here today?"
"What's the most important thing that I could cover in today's session?"
"Anything you're looking forward to hearing from me today?"

Ordinary presenters blend in. They might huddle away from their audience as they enter the room, or hide behind their lectern for the duration, or stare at their screen for an hour. You don't want to blend in, you want to stand out from the crowd and really impact your audience. Go ahead, Cassie—pop the head! These performance techniques can help take your presentations from ordinary to extraordinary.

Manager's Checklist for Chapter 8

☑ Prepare to work *with* your visuals, not for them.
   - Know where you will use the blackout function, and be ready to inform your audience.
   - Use directional language to tell your audience exactly where to look.
   - Look where you want your audience to look.

☑ Make the most of your stage!
   - Get away from the furniture. If possible, have any lecterns, tables, etc., that you won't need removed.
   - Dress to avoid blending into the backdrop.

☑ Read and check in with your audience.
   - Look for verbal and nonverbal cues to ensure your audience is with you.
   - Meet and greet your attendees to start building rapport.

Stage Movement

As Shakespeare said, "All the world's a stage." (You didn't think I'd be able to leave that quote out, did you?) When it comes to presenting, that's definitely true. Whether you have a nice, big, beautiful empty stage on which to present, or a small amount of space in a dimly lit room, or a chair at one end of a conference table, that space is yours. It's your stage, and you should own it. You can make the most of any space with effective movement to help reinforce your message.

Let me introduce you to the basic parts of the stage. While you might never use these actual terms yourself (although I encourage it—they can be very helpful), I'll reference them throughout this chapter.

In a very basic sense, every stage has five major parts that you should be aware of as defined in the key terms box and illustrated in Figure 9-1.

Bear in mind, you can combine those terms as much as you like to refer to more specific stage areas. Downstage left would be the part of the stage to *your* left, closest to the audience. Upstage right would be the inverse of that. Right center is the space slightly to the right of center stage. You can be as exact as you'd like when it comes to describing stage movement.

You know that you want to use your movement, voice, and physicality as much as possible to catch the attention of the crowd. When the stage is yours, feel free to take it! You can use whatever movement you'd like to emphasize and support the content you've got to deliver.

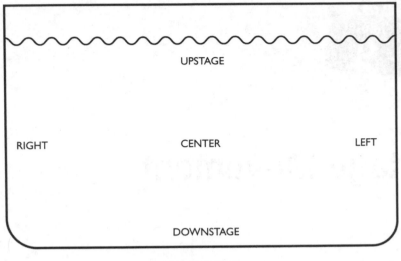

AUDIENCE

Figure 9-1. Basic parts of any stage

Upstage The part of the stage that's farthest away from the audience. This comes from the days when stages were built on an incline because the viewing seats were flat on the floor. In **KEY TERMS** order for the audience to see the people in the back of the stage, the stage needed to slope up. (Now, more often than not, it's the seating that slopes, not the stage!)

Downstage Just the opposite. Downstage is the area closest to the audience and is the inverse of the example listed above. The people at the front of the stage were easy to see, hence the stage went down.

Stage right and left The areas to *your* right and *your* left when standing onstage facing the audience. This can get tricky for some people because the directions are obviously mirrored to the eyes of the crowd. Just remember, those directions are taken from the viewpoint of the presenter.

Center Stage Just what it sounds like—the area at the middle of the stage.

Being Seen

You want to position yourself to maximize the quality of your presentation. There are a variety of techniques for doing this.

Finding Your Light

If you've ever looked up at all of the lighting instruments hanging in the air or mounted on lighting trees during a show or conference, you know that it takes numerous instruments to light one stage. Essentially, the overlapping of many separate pools of light is what brightens the entire space.

> ### SCALABILITY
>
> **TRICKS OF THE TRADE**
>
> You may be presenting on a convention center stage or in an arena or in Conference Room A down the hall. Either way, the movement we discuss in this chapter still applies. It may take you 2 steps or 20 to cross from stage left to stage right during your presentation, but don't eliminate your movement entirely. It's an issue of scale.

Because of this, there will be areas on the stage that are "hotter" (more lit, brighter) or "cooler" (less lit, darker). In order for your audience to see you optimally, you want to find the "hottest" areas of the stage. The process of finding these areas is known as "finding your light."

Take advantage of any available onstage time. If you're offered a rehearsal to check your technology, use it. Walk on the stage. Look around, and find where the brightest spot is. That's "your light." You can do this by facing the audience and feeling the heat of the lights on your face. Find the area where the light almost makes you squint but doesn't. Walk around slowly, and you'll be able to discover the brightest areas on the stage.

This is where you want to start, end, and occasionally return to during your presentation. Usually, the hottest lighting area is center stage. Center stage is a very strong position, so it often gets the most lighting attention. If this is the case, you're in luck! If not, try to find the hottest area of light near the center of the stage, and use that space.

Sight Lines

Hand in hand with finding your light is the necessary discovery of your sight lines. This will help you know how much of the stage you can use when you present. What can your audience see? Can everyone in every seat see the same thing? Who is blocked from what and where?

To figure this out, walk through the seating area of your audience. Sit down in a few seats in different places, and ask yourself what is or isn't vis-

KEY TERM

Sight lines Imaginary demarcations that indicate where the audience can see you and where they can't. On any stage, there are areas where you can be clearly seen by everyone. You're "within your sight lines." But the reverse is also true. There are locations either too far left, right, or upstage where portions of your audience will lose you. Then you are "outside of your sight lines." You always want to stay within your sight lines.

ible to you. Make a mental note of your sight lines.

Have you ever gotten an "obstructed view" ticket at a concert? If you have, you'll know that those seats usually have some sort of obstacle between you and the stage, making it difficult for you to see everything. Those obstacles change the sight lines on stage.

Are there any "obstructed view" seats for your presentation? If so, see if moving the obstacle is an option. If it's something like a leftover piece of equipment or an unused table, you may be able to have it taken away. If it's something like a large pillar or other structural feature, make sure you don't spend an extended amount of time in the area onstage that is affected by that obstructed sight line. Otherwise, you'll be out of view of a large portion of the crowd.

Confident First Impressions and Final Moments

You want to make a first impression that shows your confidence and inspires the audience's confidence in you. You also want to finish up with flair that reinforces what you've said. Here are some techniques for doing that.

Hit Your Mark

Sometimes I see a person introduced who then strides across the platform *while* saying her name *and* the first lines of her presentation *and* displaying her first visual. This is a weak opening. What are we supposed to look at? Listen to? Her name was what again? Is it starting? The solution comes from the film world. It's called "hit your mark."

It can be a challenge for some to walk in silence to the place where they are going to present, but remember this moment is also for the audience. It's a moment for them to focus in, to look up from their devices, to

> ### WALK, BREATHE, SMILE, TALK
> To hit your mark, use these four steps at the top of your presentation: walk, breathe, smile, talk.
> 1. Walk to the place you will begin.
> 2. Breathe to center yourself and support your voice. Find your **TOOLS** strong Neutral Position.
> 3. Smile to welcome the audience and start building a connection.
> 4. Talk—begin your presentation.

wonder what's going to happen next, and to connect with the person who's going to be leading the room.

> ### STRONG BEGINNINGS IN ANY SETTING
> **SMART**
> Don't lose a strong opening opportunity when presenting with your team simply because you're in a smaller, less formal environment. Say you're sitting around a conference table—the essence of this idea still holds true. To hit your mark in that situation **MANAGING** means taking in the people around you with a smile and a pause (again giving them a chance to put down their devices) and then beginning.

As the saying goes, "You never have a second chance to make a good first impression." Hitting your mark helps you do just that. But what about a final impression? Luckily, the solution is simple: end as you begin. When you've found that great area of light near center stage, return there to deliver your conclusion. Hit your mark again, and stay where you are. Stand in your strong Neutral Position, and address the crowd directly. Smile and take a breath at the end. Let the audience take in the wonder of the glorious you and your great presentation.

Using Your Stage

As I mentioned in Chapter 2, movement creates visual interest and engagement. It helps you support and enhance your message by utilizing your full body/voice connection. But it can also help your audience remember details or follow along in a complicated process. Spontaneity is great. But if you haven't gotten comfortable with the basics of effective movement, you run the risk of wandering. Like a director staging a show, pre-plan some of your big moves for a polished, professional look.

KEY TERM **Blocking** How those in theater and film refer to the preplanned movement, developed through rehearsal, that ends up in any given play or movie. Most of the time, any movement you see in either medium, sometimes down to the smallest of head turns, may be completely preplanned.

Your Most Powerful Position

As I mentioned previously, center stage is an incredibly powerful location. You command the entire space from center stage. However, there's an even stronger version of center stage for your presentation, and that's downstage center. When you stand downstage center, you are still in the middle of the stage but as close as possible to your audience.

Assuming downstage center is well lit, this is where you'll want to start and finish your presentation. This gives you a confident beginning and ending location. You might be thinking, "If this place is so strong, why don't I want to stay here the entire time?" The answer is simple: if you stay in any position, no matter how powerful, for too long, it will start to get visually boring for your audience.

A Baseball Story

FOR EXAMPLE I often talk about the three major cities in which I've lived when I give a presentation. I grew up in Baltimore, spent many years in New York City, and now reside outside of Boston. When I do this, I like to tell the tale of my baseball fandom throughout the years.

In my telling, I block the points of my story along the stage: the Baltimore Orioles center stage, the New York Yankees stage right, and the Boston Red Sox stage left (Figure 9-2). My story begins and ends with my undying love for the Orioles (Go, O's!), so while I may progress through the mentions of other teams, I return downstage center every time I mention the Orioles.

This serves a dual purpose: it helps my audience learn (and remember!) a little more about me and retains their interest by literally keeping the story "moving." Home run.

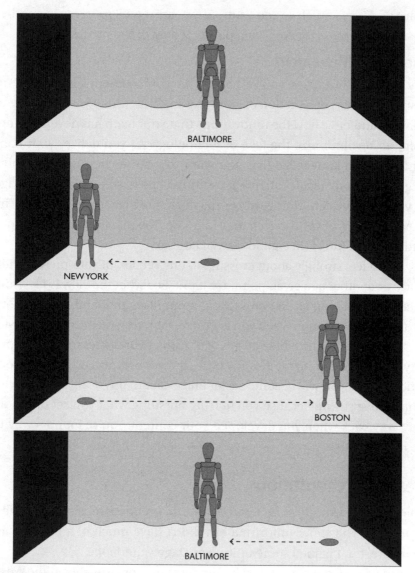

Figure 9-2. A baseball story

Movement for a List, Timeline, or Story

You can use your stage space to outline a group of items in people's mind, and pack even more punch into your stories, by using blocking. Choose which elements to underline with movement. Then, you'll cross to one stage location, land in your Neutral Position, and discuss one particular point or date as much as you want. Afterward, you'll progress to another position to discuss the following point, or step in the process, etc.

Tactic-Led Movement

Say one of the tactics you've chosen in your content creation is "to inspire." You've got a section of your presentation where you are going to tell your audience how the innovations that your team has developed are going to revolutionize the face of technology. As you deliver your content, with the knowledge that you want to inspire your audience, how might your body react? You might be compelled to step as far downstage as you possibly can. Your gestures may become bigger and sharper. The pace and pitch of your speech may increase. You're really coming at your audience full force! (In a good way, of course.)

If you feel strongly about crossing to one section of your presentation space or another at a given point, try it out. See what the view is like from over there. As long as you cross with a purpose, and land back in your strong Neutral Position when you get there, that movement could be a win.

The more comfortable you get with using your tactics to inform your physicality, the simpler it gets to come up with creative, original presentation blocking. It will become easier and easier to physically engage with what you're saying because you're truly pursuing what you set out to do way, way back when you developed your content. You've found a way to tie it all together.

Seated Presentations

I had the opportunity to be a part of a world premiere musical in La Jolla, California. The show, unfortunately, didn't have much of a life after its premiere, but I gained some unique onstage experience.

I played a woman who, just before intermission, was shot at the Western Wall in Israel. In Act II, my character was wheelchair-bound, recovering in the hospital. In one scene, I was wheeled on stage by a nurse. My character couldn't move, she/I had just been shot in the leg. However, I still had to sing a lengthy, dramatic, gut-wrenching song about the difficulties of spending many years as an undercover spy.

I needed to stay planted in that chair (after all, I had just been shot in the leg), but I still was able to keep my body engaged. I used strong gestures, leaning forward for a phrase or turning to the side. Being stuck in that wheelchair in one spot didn't stop me from using all of my body that I could.

I know that many of you spend a lot of time giving seated presentations. Just because you're sitting down doesn't mean you should allow your body to switch off! Maintain a strong seated Neutral Position. While there isn't any blocking, per se, for seated presentations, you'll want to rehearse physically just as much as you would an "on-your-feet" presentation.

PLEASE STAND; NOW BE SEATED

TRICKS OF THE TRADE

Even if you're presenting while seated, use your walk-through to get up and move. What's your body naturally doing while standing? What are those movements doing to your voice and your gestures? Now, take a seat, and "walk through" again while seated. Keep the same volume in your voice. Use the same gestures you used during your standing walk-through. Get that energy level into your muscle memory, and it will carry over in your seated presentation.

Stage movement shows a confident command of your space, and a thoughtful, prepared approach. It also keeps your audience interested, on track, and engaged. Remember, your stage is *your* stage.

Manager's Checklist for Chapter 9

☑ Your presenting space is *yours*. Whether big or small, use it to your advantage
  ■ Learn, and use, the most powerful and interesting parts of the stage.

☑ Make sure that you can be seen!
  ■ Find your light by walking the stage.
  ■ Discover your sight lines by walking through the audience.

☑ Create a strong, confident first impression and closing.
  ■ Remember to hit your mark both times.
  ■ An easy way to remember "hit your mark"? Walk, breathe, smile, introduce.

☑ Find your stage movement.
- Block your presentation ahead of time.
- Develop ways to use blocking to outline a process, a timeline, or a story.
- Experiment with the principles of tactic-inspired movement.

☑ Activate your seated presentations.
- Even though you may not leave your seat for the duration, you need to keep your physicality engaged.
- Continue to do a walk-through on your feet, at least once, to carry physical energy into your presentation.

Chapter

10

Actors' Secrets for Sharing the Stage

In any show or film, there are actors with varying levels of experience and training. Some have lofty degrees from the best programs, have performed on notable stages throughout the world, and have honed their craft over many years of hard work, attention to detail, and discipline. Others may be fresh out of college or new to the medium or have little to no experience or training at all. One isn't better than the other—both groups have much to contribute—but they have vastly different skill sets.

Actors know that any production is only as good as its weakest link, so it behooves everyone to work together and make each other look good. The very same holds true for your group presentation. Regardless of the experience of your copresenters, everyone will have something vitally important to offer.

Preparing to Copresent

Whether you're presenting with one other person or 10 people, you can make the best use of everyone's valuable time and highlight each speaker's unique skill set with some preplanning. Your preparation will take two major forms:

- Your predevelopment decisions, and
- Your presentation rehearsal.

Let's assume, for our purposes, that everyone is aware of the major key points of your presentation; when it comes to creating your actual content, you can still use the Blueprint and the objectives and tactics approach covered in earlier chapters.

When you come together for your first meeting, the primary order of business should be a decision on major objectives. Might this change over the course of your presentation development? Sure. But in your first meeting, your goal should be to decide on the major big ideas you will cover and divvy up the overall responsibilities of your presentation.

YOU DO THAT, AND I'LL DO THIS

There's preparation, and then there's preparation. In order to ensure that you are truly laying the groundwork for your "cast," don't be tempted to shortcut your preparation discussion. Make sure you're doing more than just saying "you do that, and I'll do this." The more specific you can be while splitting up presenting duties, the easier your collective jobs will be on presentation day.

To specifically split up presentation responsibilities, create a Group Blueprint. This will be the final word on your presentation content. You can do this one of two ways:

1. Each presenter can create his or her own Blueprint separately. Then, the group can meet and synthesize everyone's ideas into one Blueprint.
2. Or, you might want to create one Blueprint from the beginning that gets passed around for group development. When everyone is happy with the final product, that's the Blueprint to use.

Getting Everyone in the Right "Role"

Before anyone gets into his or her individual presentation development, you'll want to plan, as a group, who will tackle which parts of your presentation. This is the time to clarify whether or not anyone has been specifically tasked with any certain sections, if anyone is very passionate about one area, and/or if anyone wishes to highlight his or her specific strengths.

Start the discussion with these questions:

Has anyone been assigned a section head of time? You may have a subject matter expert or content superstar on your team who's been asked by higher-ups to present a specific set of knowledge. If so, discover that in your first meeting. Those people should be free to run with that content specifically.

Is anyone especially passionate or knowledgeable about a certain section of content? Have someone on the team who is dying to tackle your Q&A? Or that has built his entire career around a certain idea you need to share? Or who shines when it comes to being an emcee? Encourage your copresenters to share what they feel really passionate about in regard to the content. As humans, we devote more time and attention to things that we really care about. Give your copresenters (and yourself) the opportunity to step into a role in which they will really shine.

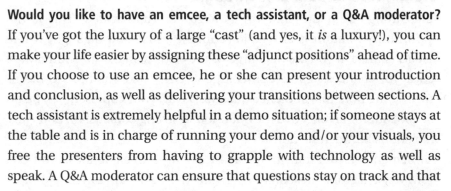

CHECK FOR "NO-GOS" SMART

MANAGING

Give everyone the opportunity to speak up if there is any part of this group presentation that they definitely want to avoid like the plague. Simply outlining the strengths of your copresenters ensures that everyone is working to the best of their abilities.

Would you like to have an emcee, a tech assistant, or a Q&A moderator? If you've got the luxury of a large "cast" (and yes, it *is* a luxury!), you can make your life easier by assigning these "adjunct positions" ahead of time. If you choose to use an emcee, he or she can present your introduction and conclusion, as well as delivering your transitions between sections. A tech assistant is extremely helpful in a demo situation; if someone stays at the table and is in charge of running your demo and/or your visuals, you free the presenters from having to grapple with technology as well as speak. A Q&A moderator can ensure that questions stay on track and that

ORGANIZING "SMALL-CAST" PRESENTATIONS SMART

MANAGING

If your copresentation is only a cast of two, asking these questions and assigning these roles still applies. Bear in mind that you both will assume more than one role. However, you can do things like alternate sections between you so that one person presents while the other runs technology, give one person the responsibility of the introduction and conclusion while the other handles the Q&A, etc. You need to be as specific with a two-person presentation as you are with a "large-cast" presentation.

audience concerns are heard. (The next chapter covers everything you need to know, and more, about Q&A.)

Group Presentation Rehearsal

After your initial meeting, everyone will (most likely) go their own way to develop their content. If you're able to check in periodically, do so. However, the big work, the work that will make your presentation shine, will come in the form of your group rehearsal.

Keep in mind, as I always say about rehearsal: it's time-flexible. If your copresenters are traveling to a conference from points around the globe, and you'll all only be able to meet in person for a half hour before you take the stage, that's OK—but *definitely* take advantage of that time. The more group rehearsal time you can schedule, the better.

If your group can only rehearse remotely prior to your presentation, at a minimum, have everyone talk through the presentation at least once. Encourage each presenter to use the Rehearsal Process on his or her own.

Group Presentation: Talk-Through

Talk through your presentation as a group while seated. This is the opportunity to address any major content issues and highlight where visuals change. If you are in charge of the visuals, make sure you notate "cues" for changes. If you're in charge of Q&A, take the time to brainstorm some potential audience questions with your copresenters. Be on the lookout for an effective introduction, a strong conclusion, and clear transitions between sections.

Remember, your transitions can be as simple or elaborate as you like. However, in a group presentation, an effective transition can be as simple as saying, "Now that we've covered that point, Elizabeth is going to introduce you to the system." If you're the emcee, note when a section will end, and be ready to say something like, "Thank you, Nick. Elizabeth will now introduce us to the new system." What makes a transition work is that it's clear, preplanned, and actually *done*.

Group Presentation: Walk-Through

Here's where things will get interesting. There are tons of aspects of stage movement that you can use in your presentation, whether it's a solo, duo, or group presentation. But, when you walk through your content, this is where you want to really get into being the director. Two major concepts can help you address stage movement in a group presentation: *where people are looking* and *where people are moving*.

> ### INTRODUCING ... (THE EMCEE TRICK)
> **TRICKS OF THE TRADE**
>
> As kind humans, we want to look at a person when introducing him or her. However, if you're functioning as the emcee for your group , your focus needs to go elsewhere. Speak the introduction to the audience, not the person you are introducing, so the person's name (or other distinguishing facts you wish to share) doesn't get swallowed up.

Look Where You Want the Audience to Look 2.0

All of the presenters should always, *always* be focusing on the person who is speaking, unless the speaker would like them to look elsewhere. (This goes for the tech assistant, as well. Any time she isn't running technology, her eyes should be on the speaker.) However, as a general rule: every eye on stage should always be focused on the speaker.

The reason for this is simple. The audience wants to become involved with whatever is holding the attention of everyone on the stage. And heaven forbid someone onstage is distracted by something else! If you break that consistent onstage focus, the audience's eyes will be drawn to whoever isn't doing what the rest of the group is.

> ### NOW, LOOK OVER HERE!
> **TRICKS OF THE TRADE**
>
> If the speaker is trying to direct the audience's eyes to a visual, all the eyes on stage should look there, as well. As the speaker, if you tell the audience to look at a certain place, give your copresenters and your audience a second to find that spot for themselves.

Group Staging

In a solo presentation, you know that you want to use your movement, voice, and physicality as much as possible to catch the attention of the crowd. The same goes for a group presentation. When the stage is yours, feel free to take it! You can use whatever movement you'd like to emphasize and support the content you've got to deliver. And you'll be able to do so because the rest of your copresenters will take advantage of the concepts of upstage and downstage.

In a group presentation, the speaker should (most often) position himself downstage and the rest of the group upstage. Depending on the number of copresenters, you can split them in two groups (stage left and right, Figure 10-1), or arrange them in a line behind the speaker (Figure 10-2). Either way is fine, as long as they are upstage enough for the speaker to use as much of the downstage area as possible. When speakers change, the current speaker and the upcoming speaker should swap positions.

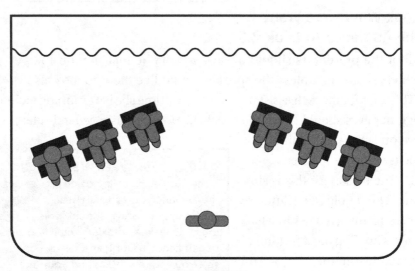

AUDIENCE

Figure 10-1. Two-group option for stage layout

TRICKS OF THE TRADE

PLEASE BE SEATED

If your presentation is longer than 10 to 15 minutes, arrange to have seats for those not speaking. You can place them in a line upstage of the speaker, or arrange them in two separate groups or even diagonally toward an upstage speaker, if lighting demands it. But whichever you choose, allowing those not speaking to sit not only gives more attention to the speaker, but also helps save the energy of those who present later. Even the best of us will start to fidget and draw focus if left standing for too long.

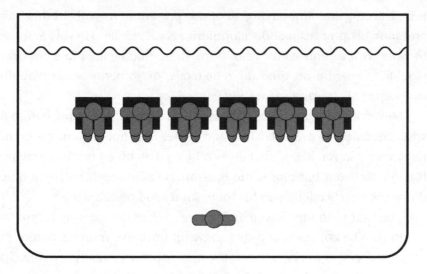

AUDIENCE

Figure 10-2. Upstage line option for stage layout

Finding Group Movement Through Dress Rehearsal

Now is the time you'll want to think about sight lines. Make sure that whoever is speaking at any given time can be seen by everyone in the audience. Have a member of the group sit in various sections of the audience while another person walks around the stage. This will help establish any sight line issues you may face.

In a group presentation, it's less important for the audience to see the waiting speakers; the current speaker is the main event. If you find you've got a tight space and you need to take advantage of a stage area that may be outside of audience sight lines, do so by placing the waiting speakers in that area.

When it is your turn to speak, all of your good presentation skills still apply to your moment on stage. Couple that with effective support from your copresenters and your audience will be blown away by your focus, professionalism, and attention to detail.

Copresenting with Someone Who Wants to "Wing It"

I was working with a longtime client, Steven, to prepare him for an upcoming speaking engagement at a conference. Steven spent a lot of time learning and embodying all of the presentation skills in this book and took his professional development *very* seriously. He was assigned to work with a copresenter who didn't share that feeling. The coworker wouldn't show up on time for rehearsals, or sometimes, he wouldn't show up at all. It was a frustrating few weeks.

Steven and I arrived at his presentation venue the evening before he was scheduled to present. The copresenter was nowhere to be found. Regardless, Steven had a great dress rehearsal on his own. We videotaped it and watched it back for some last-minute adjustments. After a quick dinner, Steven headed up to his room for a good night's sleep.

The next morning, Steven and I were back in the meeting room, raring to go. The copresenter didn't show up until five minutes before the presentation was to begin, when the audience was already arriving. The copresenter made a beeline for me and said, "Steven tells me you're a professional, so tell me what to do." I offered the only sage advice I could in that moment: "Please sit down when you're not speaking, and look at Steven any time he is speaking." I clearly couldn't improve that speaker in that moment, but I could try to set Steven up for success. Happily, Steven did a stellar job that day. The fact that he was well rehearsed made up for all the missteps of his copresenter.

What can you do if you find yourself with a copresenter who wants to avoid preparation altogether? There are things you can do to encourage your copresenter to rehearse and make everyone look good, yourself included.

Make it easy for copresenters: You've got all of this knowledge (and soon, experience!) with the Rehearsal Process and presentation preparation. The "wingers" may feel they don't have time, or they don't know where to begin. They might not feel rehearsal is really necessary. But you know different, don't you? Make it easy for reluctant copresenters. Reserve a space for presentation rehearsals, and see if you can get them to commit to at least one. Send them an invite, and tell them everything is set to go. Remember, the Rehearsal Process is flexible, so there's no need to overwhelm them with a large time commitment. A 30-minute session can make all the difference in the world.

Obviously, you can't force colleagues to do something they don't want

---

WHAT THE HECK WAS THAT?

TRICKS OF THE TRADE

Actors like to keep things fresh and new for every audience. While a performance should be alive, and change by shades from audience to audience, it should never be *entirely* different night to night.

The same should be true in a copresenting situation. No one wants to be left on a presentation stage thinking, "What the heck was *that?*" when a copresenter goes rogue. It can destroy everyone's focus, as well as hinder the relationship with your audience, based on how well that "new business" is received.

---

to. However, it's good for all of you if everyone is well rehearsed. Help them out and take the lead in scheduling.

Relegate and delegate; should this person still not want to prepare or prep with the group, try to minimize any potential damage. Sure, she may be a great presenter, but as we've established in this chapter, it's a group effort! If she doesn't have a care in the world about which section she presents, try to pass her a brief one. Go for one in the middle of the presentation; should she crash and burn, you and your copresenters can recover and still finish strong. If there are any presentation responsibilities you think she may not be able to handle on the fly, delegate that additional responsibility to someone else in the group.

If you tell such a presenter only one thing before the presentation (and let's hope that's not the case!), make sure she knows to look where she wants the audience to look to allow the speaker to shine.

It's incredibly difficult if one of your copresenters wants to go rogue and "just wing it." When all is said and done, remember to make your own presentation sections the best they can possibly be, and encourage your copresenters to do the same. The "winger" will end up looking better by default. And if she epically fails in her responsibilities, at least everyone around her will have maintained the integrity of their own performances.

Presenting on a Panel

Panel presentations can be a challenge. Often, everyone is seated at microphones behind a large table or in a line onstage. While it may be difficult to make the removal of a panel table happen (but good for you if you can!), you still want to maintain your good presentation skills as much as possible.

Presenting from the Waist Up

Just because you're behind a table or seated doesn't mean it's time to let everything go! Tables can be especially tricky because we can be tempted to slump or fold over (if we're tired) or slowly sink further and further beneath the table's edge (if we're subconsciously trying to hide). Maintain your seated Neutral Position from the waist up. Although you're seated, keep your feet placed on the floor, hips square, shoulders back, and head comfortably aligned. You'll look confident and help your voice projection stay strong.

If you're seated behind a table, make sure your hands are on the table (hands hidden below the table can look weak or like you're hiding something). Beware of banging your hands on the table when gesturing. This distracting habit could be amplified if there is a microphone on the table or on your body.

You can also use your gestures, just as you would standing up, when presenting on a panel. If you're cut off from an audience by a table, make the most of the part of your body the audience can see! Expansive, supportive gestures can go a long way toward actually connecting you with your audience. You'll catch their attention and use part of your body to "cross the divide" between you and them—the table.

CAUTION

CRUMPLED BODY, WEAKENED VOICE

Ah, the seated slump. If you fall victim to poor posture when seated, you crumple all of the anatomy you need for excellent voice projection and presence. You lessen your ability to breathe deeply, and you relax all of your supportive musculature. As a singer would on stage, try to remember to keep your strong Neutral Position (even when seated) for effective voice production.

Panel Focus

Just as with a standard group presentation, you should always, *always* be looking at the speaker. In a panel, you'll find you have quite a few of them: the moderator, an audience member asking questions, and your fellow panelists. You're all there, essentially, to have a large interactive discussion. Would you think of having a one-on-one conversation without looking someone in the eye? Absolutely not. Direct the audience's eyes to whomever is speaking, unless the speaker instructs the room to look elsewhere. ("Take a look at the upper right-hand corner of this slide.") Not only is it polite, but it makes the proceedings clear and easy for the audience to follow.

Whether you've got a "cast" of one or 10, your presentation takes preparation. The more people, the more imperative it is that you're prepared as a group. Your presentation is only as good as its weakest member. With preparation, you can take the stage with an all-star cast.

Manager's Checklist for Chapter 10

☑ With whom am I presenting?

☑ Schedule a meeting to decide who will present what.

☑ Develop content, whether separately or through collaboration.

☑ Schedule presentation rehearsal.

☑ Manage anyone who wants to "wing it."

☑ Work on panel prep. Remember, you can still be an engaging presenter, even if it's only from the waist up.

Chapter 11

Q&A Management

One of the many jobs I had while living in NYC, in between my actor gigs, was at Toy Fair—a yearly event for everyone and everything in the toy industry. Distributors and manufacturers often hire actors to demo their newest toys to potential buyers. This is where toy trends are born.

One year, I got hired to demo a new touch-and-talk fluffy animal-like creature. I was given a 60-second script that explained its unique features, and I delivered this pitch to different groups of potential buyers as they walked by on the trade show floor.

As I was saying my spiel for what felt like the millionth time that week, a large group of buyers interrupted me and started peppering me with questions, all at the same time:

"How many batteries does it take?"

"How long will the batteries last?"

"Does it sing any songs?"

"How many songs does it sing?"

"Can you make it sing along with you?"

Typically at these events, there's a representative from the toy company close by who'll step in to answer any prospect questions. However, for some reason, no one was around. It was just me, the fluff ball, and a lot of questions. I failed their inquisition miserably.

I didn't know how to answer questions well or, more important, how to *not* answer questions well. I had no idea how to control my audience, and I'm pretty sure I stood there saying a lot of "uhhhhhs" (Figure 11-1). This chapter will help you fare much better during the Q&A portion of your presentation than I did way back when.

Figure 11-1. This is me in a (purple) wig at Toy Fair prior to my Q&A fail.

Planning for Audience Questions

Q&A's can be daunting. There's a bit of a free-fall aspect to them; anything could happen. Think of a political candidate out stumping for an upcoming election. Q&A sessions are often the most volatile—or in a positive light, impactful—portions of their appearance. The public could say or do anything, good or bad. The candidates put a lot of forethought and planning into preparing for the Q&A. If you want to make the most of this part of your presentation, you should do the same.

> **KEY TERM**
> **Q&A** The question-and-answer portion of your presentation. It's an opportunity for your audience to ask about your content, as well as for you to go in depth with concepts of interest.

The first step in your planning is to decide when you want to invite audience questions. There are three major options: you can do so throughout your presentation, at the end of each section (usually related to each objective), or during a specific Q&A portion near your presentation's conclusion. Whichever way you choose to take questions, you must inform your audience during the Expectations portion of your introduction. (See Chapter 6.)

There isn't a right, wrong, or "best" way to go when it comes to this choice. This is truly up to you. You might have to try different styles to find the one that you're most comfortable with as a presenter. No matter what you choose, I say again: you must let your audience know the plan.

Free-Form Q&A: Inviting Questions at Any Time

Personally, I prefer inviting the audience to ask questions at any time they would like to. I think this keeps sessions interactive and exciting for me, and there's usually not a risk of leaving anyone with unanswered questions.

PROS AND CONS OF FREE-FORM Q&A

Pros

- Keeps the presentation lively, exciting, and different for you as a presenter.
- Ensures an audience member won't forget a question over the course of your presentation.
- Allows for the most interactive session.

TOOLS

Cons

- Distracts presenters who easily get derailed on a tangent.
- Rattles linear thinkers.
- Eats away at valuable presentation minutes.

Periodic Q&A: Taking Questions at the End of Each Section

This style is the hybrid of the free-form Q&A and the more controlled preconclusion Q&A. This is a good option to take if you want to "test the waters" of a free-form session but not fully commit.

Should you choose to embrace a periodic Q&A, use an additional Blueprint page to help you plan for questions on a section-by-section basis, as shown in Figure 11-2.

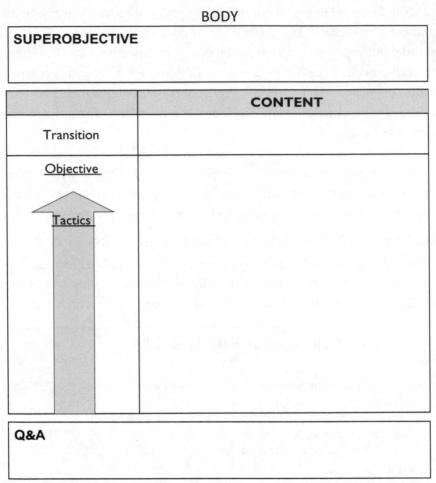

Figure 11-2. Periodic Q&A Blueprint page

Preconclusion Q&A: Leaving All Questions Until the End

I've seen way too many presenters do a stellar job with their content, give a fantastic conclusion (including a super memorable button), and then defuse all of their hard work with a postconclusion Q&A. Half their audience leaves after the button (they think that's the end!) and much of the other half tunes out entirely. For some people, the conclusion is permission to check out—whether physically or mentally. To avoid this pitfall, we recommend including the Q&A portion prior to the actual conclusion of your presentation.

PROS AND CONS OF PERIODIC Q&A

TOOLS

Pros:

- Keeps questions specific to the topic that has just been discussed.
- Ensures topic-specific questions are addressed in the moment.
- Gives an interactive feel, but you still control when that interaction happens.

Cons:

- Disrupts presentations that build to a big "payoff," like an exciting announcement.
- Invites audience to jump to conclusions and ask about concepts before they're fully introduced.
- Chips away at valuable minutes throughout your presentation.

If you're opting for a preconclusion Q&A, use an additional Blueprint page to plan and organize your thoughts (Figure 11-3).

PROS AND CONS OF PRECONCLUSION Q&A

TOOLS

Pros:

- Helps you hang on to more members of a very large audience.
- Controls audience movement, for example, if the audience needs to line up at an aisle microphone.
- Avoids presentation interruptions that may throw some speakers off-track.

Cons:

- Risks losing Q&A entirely if you begin late.
- Requires harder work to keep your audience from "tuning out" due to a smaller amount of interaction during your presentation.
- Jeopardizes your entire Q&A if content garners extreme results. Your listeners may rush to a raucous celebration, or a frustrated upheaval, and not ask any questions, period.

Of course you have the option to *not* take questions at all during a presentation. Just let your audience know. Setting the correct expectations for the audience is the key to making your Q&A, and entire presentation, a success.

	CONTENT
Transition	
Q&A	

CONCLUSION

	EXTERNAL
Transition	
Restate Agenda	
Superobjective	
Appreciation	
Button	

Figure 11-3. Preconclusion Q&A Blueprint page

Elements of a Good Answer

You've decided when to take questions. Now, *how* do you actually answer these questions? There's no specific formula you absolutely have to apply when answering a question. (I do provide one below in case formulas really work for you.) However, you do need to draw on the knowledge you have as a subject-matter expert and couple that with all the presentation skills work you've done so far. Add some—or all—of these

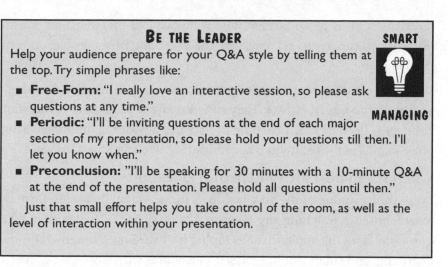

BE THE LEADER   SMART

Help your audience prepare for your Q&A style by telling them at the top. Try simple phrases like:

- **Free-Form:** "I really love an interactive session, so please ask questions at any time."
- **Periodic:** "I'll be inviting questions at the end of each major   MANAGING
section of my presentation, so please hold your questions till then. I'll let you know when."
- **Preconclusion:** "I'll be speaking for 30 minutes with a 10-minute Q&A at the end of the presentation. Please hold all questions until then."

Just that small effort helps you take control of the room, as well as the level of interaction within your presentation.

elements of a good answer, and you're on your way to an impactful Q&A.

Don't Begin with a Verbal Virus

You'll notice this book is light on "don'ts." I'm including one here because I feel that strongly about it. I want it to stick! Don't begin an answer with a Verbal Virus. Beginning your answer with a Verbal Virus immediately lowers your credibility. Your audience will start to ask themselves, "Does he really know what he's talking about?" While it's definitely part of our human condition to want to fill any silences, simply uttering filler words or sounds while thinking of an answer is far less powerful than that moment of silence itself. Here are a few things you can do instead.

Pause. Just like we discussed in Chapter 2, immediately after a question is asked, and before you speak, take a pause. You'll give your brain a chance to gather its thoughts, while maintaining credibility with your audience.

Clarify the Question If You Need To. There's no harm in making sure you're answering the actual question that's been asked. Your credibility will be diminished if you answer a question that isn't actually the one on the table, even if your answer is spot-on, perfect, and chock-full of amazing information. It may appear that you're dodging an inquiry or lacking the particulars needed to answer. A simple moment to clarify when necessary ("What I hear you asking is . . . Is that correct?") makes all the difference.

Acknowledge. "Good question," "Great question," "What an interesting question," or (my personal favorite) "Thank you for that question" are all phrases you can say to acknowledge the asker and buy a few seconds of thinking time.

Pause, Clarify, and Acknowledge are tools to help you avoid "umming" your way through an answer. They can also give a good structure to your comments during Q&A. Take time to rehearse answering questions using one—or all—of the techniques above, and see what feels best for you.

When It's Important to Repeat a Question

I was sitting in one of the very last rows of the Wang Theatre in Boston, Massachusetts, watching my favorite National Public Radio host take questions from the audience after taping his live show. This guy is funny, charming, and smart. Sadly, I missed most of his witty answers because I was so preoccupied trying to figure out what he'd been asked.

The Wang is a *huge* theater, and he was only taking audience questions from the people in the orchestra section. For him, it made sense: it's a gigantic space, and Mr. Radio Host wanted to actually hear what he was being asked.

From up in the "nosebleeds," all I could discern of the questions was muffled talking. I knew there was a question but couldn't make out a single word. At one point, Mr. Radio Host called on an audience member and intently listened to the question. Took a dramatic pause. Smiled. And said, "No." The orchestra section erupted in uproarious laughter. My fellow "nosebleed" audience members looked bewildered and disappointed. Mr. Radio Host had let us down.

The questioner wasn't thinking about the rest of the audience. He didn't care if the people in the "cheap seats" (read: me) could hear the question. He just wanted to listen to what his favorite radio host had to say. It was the responsibility of Mr. Radio Host to repeat the question so the rest of the audience could hear, understand, and appreciate it.

As the presenter, your job is the same. Take control, and repeat questions that might be missed in a large (or acoustically difficult) space. If you only remember one thing from this chapter, please remember to *always* repeat the question in such a situation.

Repeating the question may feel a little awkward at first, so it's a tech-

BUT WAIT! THERE'S MORE ...

For the most part, repeating the question applies when you're presenting to a medium- or large-sized audience. This is something you do solely for your audience's understanding and enjoyment. Or ... is it?

There's a bonus benefit to repeating a question: you get a few extra moments of "thinking time" to formulate your answer. Also, this may in turn clarify the question as well. Trust me, audience members will let you know if the question you repeated back isn't the one they want answered.

TRICKS OF THE TRADE

nique you want to practice. However, it's the number one thing that you can do during a Q&A to make a more positive impact on your audience.

Answer to All

As sincere presenters, our instincts are to answer the question that was asked of us by speaking directly to the person who asked it. If you're

EFFECTIVE QUESTION REPETITION

FOR EXAMPLE

Audience Member: Kerri, you talk about rehearsal a lot. Roughly how much time did you take to rehearse for today's presentation?

Me: Thank you for that question. This gentleman said I talk about rehearsal a lot and asked roughly how much time I took to rehearse for today's presentation.

having a one-on-one conversation, this makes sense. When you're answering questions to a group of two or more, you need to answer to all.

ARISTOTLE CAN HELP

It's Aristotle himself who's been credited with the concept of "Tell 'em what you're gonna tell 'em, tell 'em, tell 'em what you told 'em." (OK, maybe he didn't use those exact words ...) Put another way, it means that when answering a question, you first give the broad answer, second, go into more detail about that broad answer, and third, sum up what you've just said.

TOOLS

When done well, use of this formula can be very impressive. It can make it seem that the speaker has spent significant time considering the just-asked question, when in reality, she's using a technique to help her prepare in the moment. It gives you an immediate structure you can follow and buys you some thinking time, as well.

However, done poorly, this technique looks patently formulaic and makes it seem like you're trying to sell somebody something. If you're going to use it (you guessed it): rehearse it.

After you've clarified or repeated the question as necessary, the goal is to present your answer to the entire audience. If you're speaking in front of a large crowd, you'll probably give very little direct eye contact and attention to the person who asked the initial question. You won't need to work hard to hold his attention, since he wants to know your answer. He'll continue to look at you and listen to you. You want to include the rest of the room in your answer rather than exclude those who are just listening to your Q&A.

TAKE IT TO EVERYONE

Remember, when you answer to all, you've got to actually connect with the whole room! Use good eye contact with different sections of your audience, open gestures that welcome the room, and volume loud enough to fill the entire space. Don't leave anyone out.

Your job now, in addition to answering the question that was asked, is to continue to engage your audience. When you answer to the entire group, you do just that. As a result, you should reduce the number of people "tuning out" during Q&A.

Check for Understanding

For the sake of argument, let's say that now you've presented your answer using some or all of the elements above. Terrific job, well done! Next, we need to ensure that the question has indeed been answered. We do so by simply asking the questioner "Does that answer your question?"

Hopefully you'll receive a resounding "Yes!" and you can move on to the next question or portion of your presentation. If you do get a "No," you can take another stab at answering the question, ask for further clarification, or offer the unsatisfied audience member another solution.

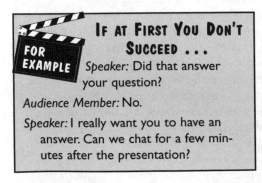

IF AT FIRST YOU DON'T SUCCEED . . .

Speaker: Did that answer your question?

Audience Member: No.

Speaker: I really want you to have an answer. Can we chat for a few minutes after the presentation?

To Ask, or Not to Ask

CAUTION

There may come a time when you don't want to check for understanding. This could be because you've received a combative question, or you're being drawn down a path you don't want to tread, or you're running short on time. You don't have to check for understanding each and every time. It is up to you as a presenter. Remember, this is your show, and you control the audience.

How to Not Answer a Question

You may get questions that you don't want to answer or, because of legal or disclosure reasons, you simply can't answer. The key to handling this situation is acknowledgment with a simple, truthful response. You must recognize the question in some way or you'll keep getting that same question. You may be perceived as dodgy, dishonest, or inauthentic.

If you can't answer the question for legal/disclosure reasons, state the truth: "I can't answer that question for legal reasons."

If you don't know the answer, admit it with a resolve: "I don't know the answer to that, but I can do some research and get back to you." Or, you can throw the question back to the audience and facilitate a discussion: "What do you think about that question? Does anyone have any thoughts?"

If the question is about something you'll cover later in your presentation, keep it simple: "I'll be covering that later."

If the question is off-topic, whether unrelated to the subject or not of interest to your entire audience, offer to take it off-line: "Let's discuss that later," or "Send me that question, and we'll set up some time to talk."

The important thing to remember is that you absolutely do *not* have to answer every single question—but you do need to acknowledge them.

Rehearsing Q&A

While you can't anticipate every single question that's going to be asked of you, you can probably make some pretty good educated guesses. This is one of the tasks in your Audience Analysis, so at this point, you already have a list of possible questions you may receive. Use these for your rehearsal. Have a colleague read the questions out loud, one at a time, and practice answering each question with the guidelines laid out in this chapter.

Keep in mind, this approach shouldn't make your answers sound stodgy or overrehearsed. On the contrary, the more comfortable you are with some of the ins and outs of the question, the more you can open yourself up to spontaneity in the moment. Whatever you do, avoid the urge to cut corners in your rehearsal by simply saying, "Oh, then I'll say something like this or this." Actually give the answer. The more intangibles you can remove from the equation, the better.

WHAT MIGHT THEY ASK?

If you've done a thorough Audience Analysis, brainstorming audience questions should be a breeze. Need a little help getting started? Get the ideas flowing with these:

TOOLS

- What might they want to know more about?
- What is a big hot-button issue?
- Are there any points of contention?
- Anything that might require further clarification during the Q&A portion?
- What's the big surprise in your presentation?

The more specific your audience questions, the better. This helps you take even more of that free-fall feeling out of your Q&A.

Once you've practiced the questions you've brainstormed, take it one step further. Ask a colleague to provide you with some tough questions that may arise. They can be related to your industry, or not. The goal is to stretch your impromptu speech muscles a bit. You want to make sure they're all warmed up for the actual presentation.

Every point in your Rehearsal Process should include some level of Q&A preparation. It's that important. Remember, you're not memorizing prepackaged answers. You should be familiarizing yourself with what may occur in your Q&A to allow for some magic when you're on your feet.

Manager's Checklist for Chapter 11

☑ Plan your Q&A process.
- Decide when you will take questions.
- Inform your audience during the Expectations portion of your introduction.

☑ Construct effective answers.

- Pause to avoid Verbal Viruses.
- Clarify, acknowledge, and repeat questions as necessary.
- Answer to everyone in the room, not just the asker.
- Check for understanding.

☑ Be prepared to *not* answer.

- Acknowledge all questions.
- Be honest with your reason for not responding.

☑ Rehearse your Q&A as you do the rest of your presentation.

- Use the questions you came up with during your Audience Analysis to prepare.
- Ask a colleague for additional tough questions.
- Build enough comfort with potential questions, but avoid memorization.

What If ... ?

This book has prepared you well. Through the Rehearsal Process you've taken as many unknowns away from your presentation as possible. But even in the most prepared scenario, there are still lingering external unknowns we can't possibly have control over. This chapter addresses some of those external "What ifs?" and suggests how to best handle them.

What If ... You Need to Acknowledge an Issue to the Crowd?

Regardless of what that issue may be, there's an overarching key to handling anything that comes your way: don't apologize to your audience. (Remember, there aren't many "don'ts" in this book, so this must be important!) When problems arise, you can confidently steer them in a different direction, you can highlight one piece of information more and give less time to another, you can take a quiet moment to deal with a technical hang-up before moving on, but apologizing will not present you in the best light. Audiences know things happen. We're all human. Most people are pretty forgiving, especially if you're honest with them about what's going on, and they don't feel like you're trying to cover anything up. They love to see someone succeed over adversity, too! But don't confuse acknowledging an issue with begging forgiveness. Opt for

"Kindly give me a moment while I deal with this gorilla that has just jumped on stage. Thank you for your patience," rather than, "Oh my gosh! I'm so sorry this gorilla, over which I have no control, has jumped on stage! Forgive me!"

What If ... You're Presenting Someone Else's Content?

This situation comes up a lot. Your boss is on vacation, you've just been moved into a new role, there's a last minute schedule change, and you have to deliver somebody else's presentation. In this situation, you're skipping over the content development part of the process. But what you're not going to skip over is the Rehearsal Process and the opportunity to make this content your own.

You still need to identify the superobjective, objectives, and tactics for this presentation as if this content were your own from the beginning. You need to take these steps as they'll still inform the words that you say out loud. Don't skimp on any of these steps.

The talk-through is essential when the content isn't your own. This is when you're going to have to really step into the mindset of an actor. You've essentially been given somebody else's words to say, and you need to be as comfortable saying them as if they were your own. You may have to talk through this material multiple times to find the connections between key points.

From there, continue the Rehearsal Process (the walk-through and the

---

CAUTION

PRESENTING MEANS NEVER HAVING TO SAY YOU'RE SORRY

When presenting on behalf of somebody else, or delivering somebody else's material, there's *still* no need to apologize. Unless you are specifically instructed to do so, for whatever reason, just begin the presentation as if it is your own. Starting with, "I'm sorry Mandy couldn't be here" lowers your credibility with regard to your command of the information and may distract your audience from you. They may be sitting there thinking "Hmmm, what is Mandy doing today?"

dress rehearsal) just as you would for any other presentation. The important piece of homework here is identifying your objectives and tactics.

What If ... You Don't Care about or Aren't Connected to the Content?

This is one of the top questions I get asked when I'm facilitating or coaching. Know that if this comes up for you in your professional life, you're not alone. In fact a lot of actors feel this way about material that they're performing, as well. Thanks to their training, it's doubtful that you'd ever be able to tell.

So, what can you do if you don't care about the material? What if you're just not connected to your content? The simple answer is, you have to get there. You have to find something that you resonate with, or you might as well not show up. You could just send a written outline of what you would've said, and the delivery impact would be about the same.

Remember that the presentation isn't about you; it's about your audience. If the content itself doesn't excite you or isn't fun for you to talk

---

ASK THE RIGHT QUESTION   SMART

A client requested our assistance to select which of his employees should present at the next big product launch. We used the opportunity to not only "audition" prospective speakers, but to educate them as well. We ran a mini presentation skills class that MANAGING taught the essentials and allowed us to identify who had strong potential to be a star. The decision came down to two young managers who were energetic and likable. The client asked me for my recommendation, so I requested a brief one-on-one meeting with each of them. I asked them one simple question: Do you want this opportunity?

This was a big commitment. It was a few weeks of long rehearsal days, global exposure, and adapting to constant script changes.

Speaker A said "Yes, I do. I know how much work this is going to be and it will take time away from my job and family. But the idea of being the spokesperson for the launch is really exciting."

Speaker B said "I think it will be good for my career."

I recommended Speaker A for the job.

As a manager you need to ask the right question of your team or even yourself. When faced with presenting less desirable content, ask, "Do you (or I) want this opportunity?" If the answer is anything other than yes, it might be time to give this opportunity to someone else, if possible.

about, then the focus on your superobjective must be even stronger. It has to become all about how and what you want your audience to do. That's where you will find your enthusiasm.

What If ... You Have to Deliver the Same Information Over and Over Again?

I was working with Emily, who was in HR at a large manufacturing company. Every week, it was her job to present an hour-long time clock training to new hires and individuals who were not using the time clocks correctly. She hated this presentation. It had to be very specific, there were a lot of rules she had to get across, and she didn't feel comfortable inserting personal stories.

She needed to find a better way to deliver this information so that the audience would actually know how to use the time clock, and so neither she nor they would be bored out of their mind. She wondered if it could be something she'd look forward to every week rather than dreading it. Emily needed to find her personal motivation.

Here's how I led Emily toward it:

Me: What do you want your audience to do?

Emily: I want them to learn how to use the time clock correctly.

Me: So that they what?

Emily: So that they use the time clock correctly.

Me: OK. What happens if they don't use the time clock correctly?

Emily: The reports are wrong.

Me: Then what happens?

Emily: Then I have to fix all their mistakes.

Me: What does that look like?

Emily: I have to go to the weekly reports line by line, find discrepancies, and confirm the actual hours with the workers and their manager. Then I have to go back into the system, fix the hours, and generate another report.

Me: How much time a week would you save if every single person used the time clock correctly?

Emily: On average, eight hours.

Me: Arguably, you would save an entire day's worth of work a week if these people were able to use the time clocks correctly?

Emily: Yes, on average eight hours. An entire day.

Me: What would an entire day back in your workweek mean to you?

Emily: Well, that would mean I may be able to take lunch a few days a week, or maybe I could leave by five every day and get to the gym.

As we continued this conversation, I noticed Emily's face started to brighten and her voice even got a little higher. Her body language opened up and there was noticeable relief on her face. We had found her personal motivation! If the presentation had a more impactful delivery, then there would be less mistakes made weekly with the time clocks. This would allow her to embrace the healthier lifestyle she's been wanting.

The following week Emily delivered the presentation with her new-found personal motivation. Just before she began, as she took a breath and stood in her Neutral Position, she thought about her personal motivation. I had her visualize a healthy lunch and the door to her gym on the wall behind her audience. She called me after the presentation was over. She said that for the first time in the 10 months she'd been delivering that content, she smiled. Identifying her personal motivation, and keeping that in mind as her end goal, really helped.

To find your personal motivation, ask yourself:

What's my superobjective?

If the superobjective is achieved, what does that look like to me?

How do I benefit from the audience achieving this goal?

What If ... You Get Shorted on Time?

This happens. A lot. It's happened to me many times in many different situations. The preceding speaker goes overtime. There was a late start due to technical difficulty. There was a two-hour snow delay and everyone's session is shortened by 20 minutes. This is yet another reason why preparation is key. You have to be very familiar with your content so you can make smart decisions about what to cut when time is tight.

The easiest thing to eliminate is the part that doesn't fully involve you—the Q&A. If you're short on time and you feel it will be a detriment to the presentation to cut anything, then don't include a Q&A. Of course, this means you have to let the audience know during the Expectation portion of your introduction.

Or, you could make the decision to cut out a few details and examples and only highlight the most important information. Identify the top tier, big ideas that are essential to your subject and you want your audience to know. Be sure to offer a way to continue the conversation after the presentation is concluded.

What If ... You're Given Extra Time?

The situation is not as common, but it does happen.

You can lengthen your presentation time by extending your Q&A. There is a risk in doing this, however. You may be left with even more dead-air time if your audience doesn't have any questions. The easiest way to combat this is to take a few minutes prior to the presentation and jot down some open-ended discussion questions. That way if your extended Q&A isn't successful and no one is asking questions, you can become not only presenter but facilitator. Throw out some thought-provoking questions to the audience. Ask for different opinions, and get a good discussion going.

If the conversation gets too off-track, remember you're the presenter—you're in charge. Rein the audience back in by saying, "Thank you for those thoughts. I want to return to our main point of . . . ."

To fill extra time you can also tell an additional story. It's always a great time filler. You're now a confident storyteller, so go ahead and give it a try! Give your audience another opportunity to get to know you.

What If ... You Skip a Major Point?

Let's say you make a mistake. Congratulations, you're officially human. Depending on when you realize your mistake, you can take different courses of action to rectify the situation. If you're still presenting and you realize, "Oops, I totally skipped a section," simply finish up what you're saying and return to the point that you skipped. The key, of course, is to not say "I'm so sorry I forgot this point, I'm going back." Simply state "Let's look at this from a different angle" or "Looking back at something I mentioned before" or "Let's continue on one of my points." You want to let your audience know where you're going without apologizing. They'll follow you.

If you realize you've forgotten something after you're done, you could send a follow-up e-mail offering some additional points. Keep it simple, straightforward, and unapologetic. Or simply let it go. Remember, your audience wasn't there for your Rehearsal Process. They don't know how it was supposed to go. If your delivery was compelling and confident, a forgotten point won't even be noticed.

What If ... You Forget a Prop?

I was sitting in the audience at a conference watching one of my clients give a keynote presentation. The lights went down, the entrance music came up, and his name was announced. He walked onstage, stood confidently down-center, went into a fabulous Neutral Position, and started to tell a story as his attention grabber. Suddenly, midstory, he said, "I'm sorry, I'll be right back. I forgot my remote" and ran off stage.

His microphone was on, so the entire audience heard him fumbling and digging through things backstage. He started to sound little panicked about his missing remote. "I forgot my remote. Has anyone seen my remote? Do you know where my remote is?" These offstage antics took about 45 seconds but probably felt about 45 minutes long to him. He bounded back onstage, smiling with confidence, saying "I got it!" Without missing a beat, he continued on with his presentation.

Afterward, we sat down to debrief and talk about what would've been a better choice than apologizing to the audience about the missing remote and running off stage to get it. We came up with these solutions.

1. **Just Go Without.** His computer was onstage, so he simply could have controlled the visuals by walking over to his computer. Now this would have kept him closer to furniture, and he would not have been able to execute his well-rehearsed staging, but he wouldn't have had this awkward running-off-and-coming-back-on situation.
2. **He Could've Called It What It Was.** During his introduction, he could have said, "I'm ready to jump into my presentation, but it turns out I've forgotten my remote. Hey, can anyone backstage bring it to me?"

This is risky. Would anybody backstage be listening? Would anybody have brought it to him? However, if someone had, not only would he have his remote, but there might have even been a nice moment for a little humor: "Good thing I've got hundreds of these stashed backstage!"

3. **He Could Have Done What He Did.** Physically walk backstage to look for the remote. He could have done that and continued with his story while he was searching so the audience was at least getting part of the introduction while he was out of sight.

If it were me, I would've embraced number one. I would have gone without. No, it wouldn't have been what I'd rehearsed, but I think it's the choice that maintains the highest level of credibility.

What If ... You Totally Lose Your Audience?

If there's a big news event and everybody gets an alert on their mobile device, they may start to become distracted. If there's been a big announcement by the speaker before you that everybody's abuzz about, or a huge sporting event that's distracting the bulk of your audience during your presentation, acknowledge it. Bring it up. Talk about it. Find a way to get your audience to focus in on you, even if it's just for a few minutes before they go back to reading and discussing whatever's on the forefront of their minds.

CONFLICTING INTERESTS

FOR EXAMPLE

Say you're about to give an important presentation and it just so happens to be during the World Series. You're at a conference in Baltimore, and the Orioles are ahead. (They would be if I had my way!) You've got a lot of hometown sports fans in the crowd, and many people are consumed by the game.

To keep from losing your listeners entirely, you could try something like this: "Before we get started, I just want to see a show of hands—how many Orioles fans are here today? What a big day for the O's! Anyone know the score? Shout it out. Hey, that's great! I know it will be on your minds during the next hour, but please do your best to focus in on me as much as possible. We'll all do the wave together when I'm done!"

What If ... You Have a Heckler or a Hijacker?

The bane of stand-up comedians around the world, on occasion you may have one person in your audience who feels he simply *must* be heard. More often than not, this kind of response erupts during smaller presentations or meetings. (It takes a lot of nerve to disrupt a keynote!) It might be because hecklers disagree with your stance or they think their responses are too hilarious not to share (news flash: they're usually not) or they feel they know your topic better than you and attempt to take over your presentation. Whatever the reason, a heckler or a hijacker can be a thorn in the side of a presenter. Anyone can simply nod and laugh off a single comment. But if you're faced with persistent dissension from an audience member, call it out, and offer to talk more later: "Nick, I can see you've got a lot of feelings on this topic. I appreciate that. Can we chat more about them later on so we can cover all the content on the agenda today?" If that's not good enough, don't be afraid to politely take a stand. "I've got to ask you to hold it back a bit for the benefit of everyone else here."

Some folks with an especially quick wit might be tempted to joke back, but don't feel that you have to join in any way. Bear in mind, the heckler or hijacker may get a rise out of riling you; you don't have to give him the pleasure.

What If ... You Discover an Error in Your Visuals?

Sometimes, you may be confronted with a blemish on your visuals. This could be due to a proofing mistake on your part, or because something is just not working correctly on the tech end. There is an easy method to deal with this, which I refer to as "Acknowledge and Shut It Down." Here's a time I found it particularly useful: I was presenting in front of a pretty large group of people with my normal visuals and my well-rehearsed interactive presentation. Just before my session, the meeting planner asked me to switch rooms. She said, "Don't worry about setting up your computer, we've got one all set up with the projector. Just move your visuals over to the computer sitting on the lectern." So I did.

A few clicks into my presentation, I realized my visuals looked very different than they did on my computer. They looked kind of jumbled, as if I had built them in a very careless manner or after a couple of cocktails. Because of the room change, I didn't have an opportunity to check my visuals prior to starting.

I made the decision to acknowledge and shut it down by stating, "Despite what you may think, I did not put the slides together last night at the bar. These are being shown on a different system than they were built on, so they look a little jumbled. I'm just going to shut them down." At the end of the presentation, I offered to send the slides to anybody who requested them.

In that instance, I knew that my visuals weren't going to be able to do their primary job, which was to support me, the speaker. They were only going to detract from my information. Rather than struggle against them, the best decision was just to take them out.

What If ... You Need to Cancel?

I am very much from the school of thought that you must "keep calm and carry on," but sometimes, you have to throw in the towel. I've seen lots of successful speakers go on with sniffles, twisted ankles (make sure you have a stool readily available), and even low-grade fevers. If you're feeling confident and think you can rally through, by all means, do it.

If you're highly contagious, if you think you won't make it through the presentation without really getting sick, or you're not emotionally up for the challenge due to a major trauma in your life, then you need to cancel.

I have a longtime client, we'll call her Noreen, who was giving the closing keynote at a two-day conference. We developed content, and rehearsed for weeks. This was the big debut of a product that she'd been working on for a long time, and she was very excited. She was scheduled to fly to New York from the Midwest on Sunday (I was flying in from Boston), and we were going to rehearse Monday, before her Tuesday presentation.

Sunday morning she called me and said she had a family emergency and wasn't going to make it in Sunday night. She was now planning to arrive Monday morning.

Monday she called to say she was flying in Tuesday morning and, could we reschedule? She told me a little bit more about the situation—her husband had been taken to the hospital with a medical emergency. I told her "I admire your tenacity and your willingness to fulfill your obligation, but where's your mind going to be tomorrow? Are you really going to be able to concentrate? Will you be able to attend other sessions and talk to other people and gather the information that you need to deliver the best closing keynote possible?" She said "You're right, my mind will be in the hospital room with my husband." Together we made the decision to cancel.

Although you may not want to, once in a while you have to throw in the towel. If you choose to cancel, for a good reason, you will not lower your credibility. Going on-site, delivering a presentation that isn't done with your full mind, body, and energy will, for sure, lower your credibility and reputation as a speaker.

What If ... You Get Surprising Feedback?

Postpresentation, you may be bombarded with many, many thoughts from your audience—hopefully, all glowing accolades! If your presentation feedback is positive, enjoy it. Say thank you to those who compliment you. There's no need to ask *everyone* if there's anything they think you can improve. Save that for a select few. (Chances are, you know who they are.)

If for some reason, your feedback is unexpectedly negative, take a deep breath and take it in stride. If you can, ask for clarity from the responders ("What specifically are you referencing?" "What exactly would

YOU CAN'T BE ALL THINGS TO ALL PEOPLE

In the theater, as in life, everyone's got an opinion. Actors hear them from directors, critics, agents, managers, other actors, audiences, coaches, and more. But seasoned actors know that if they tried to change themselves based on each individual whim, not only would they lose themselves, but they'd never please everyone, no matter how hard they tried.

Most actors I know have a small circle of people whose professional opinions *do* matter to them. You might have a mentor, a past boss, or a trusted colleague you consult with when it comes to surprising feedback. While outside opinions can occasionally be valuable, make use of the network that you trust, that knows *you*. And remember, no matter what, you can't be all things to all people.

you change?"), but avoid getting defensive. Everyone's got his or her own opinion, and it's just that—an opinion. You don't have to change everything based on one person's opinion.

If you find you get an overwhelming number of certain responses ("I couldn't hear you." "I couldn't follow your logic." "Your visuals were confusing."), take that feedback to that select few mentioned above, and discuss. See if there's a way you could have improved those areas, and make a plan for next time.

We're human. Life happens. There are always going to be "what ifs" to consider. What's important is that they don't throw you. As the saying goes, the show must go on!

Manager's Checklist for Chapter 12

☑ The unexpected will arise! Remember:
  - Don't apologize.
  - Let your audience know what's happening, and deal with it calmly. Audiences can be very forgiving.

☑ You might not always be presenting your own content, or content you actually care about.
  - Rehearsal is especially important for content that's not yours.
  - You still *must* find your superobjectives, objectives, and tactics.
  - Find your personal motivation.

☑ You can always deal with too much or too little time.
  - Make sure you are so familiar with your content that you can make cuts on the fly.
  - Cutting your Q&A in a tight time situation may be the best option.
  - With extra time, you can always add a story, or extend your Q&A.

☑ If you lose your audience to a news item, or if you've got a heckler/hijacker:
  - In both situations, acknowledge what's going on.
  - If your heckler gets out of hand, don't be afraid to call him or her out.

☑ Should you find an error in your visuals, or forget a prop:
  - Keep your cool! There is a solution.

- Sometimes, the solution is shutting down visuals or doing without props.

☑ No matter what feedback you get:
  - Thank those who compliment you.
  - Remember, you don't have to take everyone's opinion into account. Use your trusted network to sort through comments postpresentation.

Putting It All Together

Let's pause, take a breath, and take a moment to review. We've gone through the foundation of presentations, the content, and the delivery. Looking at those three areas, you can see that they line up with the order and overarching ideas of the Rehearsal Process: the talk-through, walk-through, and dress rehearsal.

I want you to use the tools and ideas that will be most useful for you. For example, if you aren't that bothered by stage fright (first of all, congratulations, you're rare), then find something else to concentrate on. The chapter on fear can still help since core breathing and the Rehearsal Process can make you even better. If you know a large part of what you'll be doing soon involves Q&A, think back to that. If you've always struggled putting your presentations on their feet, go back and spend a little time on stage movement in Chapter 9. I've covered a lot of material with you, and if it feels at this point like all the pieces are on the shop floor, I would totally understand.

What now? How can you begin applying the principles in this book?

If you're truly serious about becoming a better presenter, you've got to commit your time. In fact, if there's one word I want to leave you with at the end of this book, it's *commitment*. If you've reached this page, having taken the time out of your busy life to comb through this book, you're already dedicated to the idea of improving your presentation skills. You wouldn't be here with me if that wasn't the case!

Now, take that commitment, and make it grow. Commit to learning the fundamentals of how you move, speak, and look when you present, to ensure you're communicating only what you want. Dedicate yourself to creating more thorough and active content with the Blueprint. Challenge yourself to tell *your* stories, and bring your most engaging self to the presentation stage.

And rehearse, rehearse, rehearse.

I know you can do it. Thank you for reading, and break a leg.

Appendix

Presentation Blueprints

To assist you in planning your presentation, I am including the three presentation Blueprints included in Chapter 6 that you can copy and use. I recommend that you enlarge them using that tool on your copy machine.

INTRODUCTION

	EXTERNAL
Attention Grabber	
You	
Superobjective	
Agenda	
Expectations	

BODY

SUPEROBJECTIVE	

	CONTENT
Transition	
Objective	

CONCLUSION

	CONTENT
Transition	
Restate Agenda	
Superobjective	
Appreciation	
Button	

Index

About the Author

Kerrie Garbis, President and cofounder of Ovation Communication, has trained hundreds of executives across the globe on presentation and communication skills. Her enthusiasm, humor, and energy inspire multiple repeat client engagements. Learn more about her at www.ovationcomm .com.

A professional actress since childhood, Kerri began her studies in voice and theater at The Baltimore School for the Arts before earning her BFA in Musical Theater from Syracuse University.

She has starred in productions of Evita, Singin' in the Rain, and The Lady With All the Answers (a one-woman play about Ann Landers), to name a few. You may also have seen her catching a pass from a New England Patriot, singing a Christmas carol, or complaining of bloating in a television commercial. Kerri is a member of Actor's Equity Association.